Why Am I a Jew?

Shmuel Rosner

WS
WICKED SON

A WICKED SON BOOK
An Imprint of Post Hill Press
ISBN: 979-8-89565-460-6
ISBN (eBook): 979-8-89565-461-3

Why Am I a Jew?:
A Contemporary Guide for the Perplexed

Cover Design by Conroy Accord
English Translation by Marilyn Fefer
English Editor: Jessica Kasmer Jacobs

This is a work of nonfiction. All people, locations, events, and situations are portrayed to the best of the author's memory.

Post Hill Press
New York • Nashville
wickedsonbooks.com
posthillpress.com

Published in the United States of America
1 2 3 4 5 6 7 8 9 10

To my father, my teacher; and my mother, my teacher.

> That I could be one of you, humble of the earth, mute of being, weaving your lives in secret, modest of talk and deed. Hidden dreamers, minimizers of words and maximizers of beauty…
>
> Hayyim Nahman Bialik

Hayyim Nahman Bialik, "That I Could Be One of You," in *Selected Poems of Hayim Nahman Bialik*. Ed. and trans. Atar Hadari. Syracuse University Press, 2000, 91.

Table of Contents

An Abbreviated Timeline of Jewish History: From Creation to the Present*

3761 BCE: The Creation (according to Jewish tradition; scientists insist on a different date)

1813 BCE: Abraham is born. (1,948 years after the Creation, according to Jewish tradition)

1440 BCE: Exodus from Egypt (calculated by counting back from the start of the construction of the Temple according to the Book of Kings)

1004–928 BCE: Kingdom of David and Solomon (divided into two kingdoms after Solomon)

722 BCE: The Northern Kingdom falls. (The majority of the Jewish people disappear never to return.)

586 BCE: Destruction of the First Temple (The first Babylonian Exile began more than a decade earlier.)

539 BCE: Return to Zion (Some of the Jews return under a decree by King Cyrus; the construction of the Second Temple commences in 515.)

300–70 BCE: Canonization of the Bible (a lengthy process that apparently began in the days of Ezra)

167 BCE: Hasmonean Revolt (which lasted for several years until 161 BCE)

37 BCE: Start of the reign of King Herod (whose consequences are still visible in Israel today)

26–36 AD: Crucifixion of Jesus (Although there is a lack of consensus on the exact year, one must agree that it was a pivotal event in Jewish history.)

70 AD: Destruction of the Second Temple (four years after the outbreak of the revolt against the Romans)

70–250 AD: Tannaim period (The Bar Kokhba revolt lasted from 132 to 136.)

250–500 AD: Amoraim period (According to Jewish tradition, the Talmud was compiled by Ravina and Rav Ashi in 550.)

570 AD: Muhammad is born. (He receives his first revelation in 610, dies in 632, and Jerusalem is conquered by the Muslims in 638.)

700–1250: Geonim period (Saadia Gaon completes the transcription of the Siddur [prayer book] in 940.)

1040–1105: "Rashi," Rabbi Shlomo Yitzchaki (the greatest biblical and talmudic commentator)

1096: First Crusade (The Christians launch a campaign against the Muslims and also slaughter Jews along the way.)

1138–1204: Maimonides, "the Rambam," Rabbi Moses ben Maimon (author of the Mishneh Torah and Guide for the Perplexed)

1347: Jews are blamed for the Black Death. (Pope Clement VI exonerates the Jews from causing the plague but fails to persuade the masses.)

1492: Expulsion from Spain (putting an end to 500 years of vibrant Jewish life on the Iberian Peninsula)

1516: Establishment of the Venetian Ghetto (marking the start of a new Jewish institution)

1520: Establishment of the Council of Four Lands (a milestone in turning Eastern Europe into the center of the Jewish world)

1534–1572: Isaac Luria, "The Holy Ari," (teaches Kabbalah in Safed)

1544: Martin Luther condemns the Jews. (Christian anti-semitism assumes a new form.)

1563: Shulhan Arukh (Rabbi Yosef Karo codifies Jewish law.)

1626–1676: Shabbetai Zvi (the most convincing messiah figure since the days of Jesus's disciples)

1648–1655: Chmielnicki pogroms (Tens of thousands of Polish Jews are massacred.)

1677: Baruch Spinoza dies. (the first Jew of the Contemporary period)

1700–1760: Rabbi Israel ben Eliezer, "the Baal Shem Tov," (the founder of the Chassidic movement reinvents Judaism).

1729–1786: The "Vilna Gaon," Rabbi Elijah of Vilna, (the leader of the opponents of Chassidism)

1729–1786: Moses Mendelssohn (the father of the Haskalah, the Jewish Enlightenment movement)

1776: American colonists write The Declaration of Independence. (And Jews find a home that guarantees universal freedom of religion.)

1789: French Revolution, the start of Jewish Emancipation (at least in principle, if not in practice)

1810: Reform Judaism (The first Reform temple, founded by Israel Jacobson, opens its doors in Seesen, Germany.)

1839: Moses Schreiber, "Chatam Sofer," dies. (the first Orthodox Jew)

1881–1914: Mass migrations to the United States (the rise of the largest Jewish community in the world)

1897: Theodor Herzl and the First Zionist Congress (The word "Zionism" was coined about a decade earlier.)

1939–1945: The Holocaust (The majority of European Jewry is annihilated.)

1948: Establishment of the State of Israel (mass immigrations of Jews from Muslim countries and of Holocaust survivors)

1967: Six Day War (a historic victory and the start of a political controversy)

1978: Peace treaty with Egypt (the first Arab country to recognize Israel)

1995: Assassination of Yitzhak Rabin, Israel's Prime Minister (Disputes over policy lead to violence between Jews.)

2000: A Jew runs for vice president of the United States. (Senator Joe Lieberman makes history.)

2023–2025: October 7, 2023, Hamas massacre and subsequent war (attacks are launched against Israel from Gaza, Lebanon, Iran, Iraq, and Yemen). The war continues throughout 2024 and 2025 and prompts a worldwide wave of anti-Israel and anti-Jewish rhetoric and protest. In June, Israel, with US assistance, attacks Iran's nuclear facilities.

*At best, every timeline reflects choices that suit its author and period, making them subject to interpretation and differences of opinion. This timeline was compiled using multiple sources and relied on various books and articles. As many of the dates it contains are open to debate, in several cases we chose to cite the probable period rather than a specific year. However, we have not included the list of sources here because, to a great degree, it overlaps with the sources we referred to in the book's various chapters, whose names are found in the endnotes.

A Very Short Prologue: Where Are We At?

Remember the days of old; consider the years of many generations. Ask your father and he will show you, your elders, and they will tell you.
(Deuteronomy 32:7)

This is a very short book about an ancient people blessed with a long memory.

The Jews are a people who rely on their historical consciousness more than any other nation.[1] They have learned to assume a particular form and then shed it without losing a sense of the historical continuum.[2]

Jews work their way between breakthroughs and calamities, between destruction and revival. Every jolt alters them and produces a turnabout, or at times a revolution, in their religious and political culture. But even these revolutions do not interrupt the continuum. These evolutions do not seek to erase the past and start with a blank slate—they are of continuity and change. The slaves in Egypt are not like the nomads they became in the desert, but they are the same people. The nomads are not like the conquerors they became in Canaan, but they are the same people. The conquerors are not like the residents, and the residents are not like the exiled, and the exiled are not like the dispersed, and the dispersed are not like the returned—nevertheless, they are the same people.[3]

Judaism changes in keeping with the times and circumstances in which the Jews find themselves, hopping between revolutions—whether that of Abraham or that of Moses, both perhaps only fables—who founded the Jewish people and imparted an unparalleled faith to them.[4] Afterward, during periods that have since been recorded in the annals of human history, there were more jolts, more revolutions. One was the ruin of the Kingdom of Israel, which left behind only the Judeans, later known as Jews. And there was the destruction of the First Temple, and then the first revival, and then the destruction of the Second. And there was the sage Yohanan Ben Zakkai, who offered a substitute for the ritual practices that had been the focus of Jewish life in the absence of the Temple, ushering in a new era of rabbinical scholarship.[5] And there was Judah the Prince (Rabbi Yehuda HaNasi) and Ravina and Rav Ashi, who in the cultural memory are attributed with codifying the Mishnah and the Talmud[6] and thus ratifying the conception of the Jews as the People of the Book. And the expulsion from Spain took place nearly a thousand years after the Talmud was compiled, which produced a Kabbalistic-apocalyptic reaction as well as the seeds of a secularization process.[7]

Judaism today is a product of these many revolutions, big and small.[8] It's the outcome of the few mentioned here and the many that are not. It occurred in the more distant past (the ages of Christianity and Islam) and more recently (Sabbateanism, the Enlightenment, the Jewish Emancipation). The Judaism of today is an extension of the Judaism of yesterday, but is far from a carbon copy. And, clearly, the Judaism of tomorrow won't be like the one today; the jolts persist.[9]

Changes are guaranteed because Judaism and the Jewish people are just starting to formulate their response to one of the most dramatic periods in their history. They are on the threshold of another revolution. Here is what they experienced in a brief period, in the blink of a historical eye (less than three hundred years): the undermining of their naïve faith in God and in chosen-ness; the dismantling of the traditional Jewish community, and the recognition of Jews as having equal rights like everyone else; the horrific annihilation of European Jewry; the rise of a thriving Jewish community in the United States; the liquidation of the Jewish communities in the Islamic countries, ranging from Iran to Morocco;[10] and the establishment of a Jewish national homeland in the Land of Israel for the first time since the days of the Hasmonean dynasty.[11] A state that still must fight and pay dearly, in blood, to preserve its existence.

All of the above completely transformed the condition of the Jewish people.[12]

The Jews—myself included—are still in a period of recovery and acclimation.[13] We are still processing a new existential situation. We are still shaping our image while advancing toward an unknown Jewish future. In this book's prologue, I am ready to call the current moment a crisis.

This book is a snapshot of a Jewish moment in time as perceived by a single observer. It collates multiple viewpoints regarding one passing and elusive but transformational moment.

It's an invitation to discuss the present, think about the future, and examine the past.

Volumes have been written about each of the topics the book explores. One can, and probably should, discuss each of the interpretations it suggests for years to come. This book is intentionally short, an attempt to encapsulate the current state of Jewishness.

Here, I will present a relatively broad range of options and interpretations but won't provide any definitive preference regarding most issues that arise. After all, Jews are still debating them, and no decision has been reached. The outcomes of that debate will determine how the Jewish people and Judaism take shape in the future. Well, they will decide whether Jews even have a future. Was the renowned Jewish historian Simon Dubnow right when he claimed that "Jewry, being a spiritual entity, cannot suffer annihilation?"[14] That's a chilling insight, considering it was written by someone whom the Nazis later murdered.

We'll present seven questions in seven chapters in this book, each facilitating discussion about a different issue about the state of Judaism today. The chapters are condensed, and the discussion is not exhaustive. Anyone wishing to delve into the subject can retrieve references and suggested reading from the endnotes. Anyone wishing to utilize the book for discussion or reflection can refer to the outlines of the major points at the end of each chapter.

We'll ask what Judaism is: a tough question today, as it always has been. After all, Maimonides's concept of divinity isn't similar to that of the Kabbalah, and the principles of Judaism according to Rabbi Hasdai Crescas are unlike those embraced by a contemporary Jew.[15] We'll examine who a Jew is nowadays, a question that's even more perplexing following the establishment of the State of Israel and a question that interfaith marriages worldwide complicate even more. We'll take a close look at the concept of "Jewish values," whether they even exist; we'll examine the hatred of Jews, and then the conundrum that prominent philosophers and historians are also grappling with: How have Jews managed to survive? We'll inspect Israel's role as the Jewish nation-state and reflect on the origins of Jewish genius and on the question of whether, and if so, why, Jews tend to excel.

Finally, we'll ask what mission Jews have and why it would be worth their while to continue being Jews. Why it would be worth your while to continue being a Jew.

I wish to thank the leaders of Anu—The Museum of the Jewish People, the Chair of the Board of Directors, Irina Nevzlin, and the former CEO, Dan Tadmor, for making this book possible. They are the ones who thought a book like this was needed. Believing I was a suitable person to write such a book, they persuaded me to accept the challenge. They are the ones who formulated and advanced a course of action. They also knew when to step aside, enabling me to study and research, which took longer than planned, and then sit down and write. I not only owe them my gratitude for this book but also for more than a year of fascinating work: a year during which I had the opportunity to become reacquainted, albeit somewhat differently, with the Jews.

This book was first published in Israel in 2016. It was translated into English by Marilyn Fefer and its updated version was edited by Jessica Kasmer Jacobs. Its release in English in 2025 was initiated and supported by The Jewish People Policy Institute (JPPI), a place that had been my professional home for a decade and a half.

Question 1:

What Is Judaism?

And there are three fundamental and necessary principles of the divine religion, which are: the existence of God, providence through reward and punishment, and the divine origin of the Torah.
(Rabbi Joseph Albo, "Sefer HaIkarim")[16]

He was a "Jew from Moravia."[17]

"My parents were Jews, so I've remained a Jew myself."

And then he squirmed a bit: "If the question were put to me since you have abandoned all these common characteristics of your countrymen, what is there left to you that is Jewish? I would then reply, 'A very great deal, and probably its very essence.'" That essence, he had to admit, "he could not now express clearly in words."

That Jew, whose Jewish doctrine is so tangled that it defies description, is Sigmund Freud, the father of psychoanalysis, who was of a generation of giants engendered by European Jewry in the nineteenth century and early twentieth century.[18] In some of his writings, particularly in his book *Moses and Monotheism*,

Freud's search for a key to understanding Judaism is evident.[19] The difficulty in defining Judaism is something he shared with many other Jews of his period, and our period as well. It stems from ideological distress that shook the Jewish people and has not yet been resolved.

For over two hundred years, the Jewish world has been grappling with a crisis of identity.

What's the source of that crisis? The following is an explanation in a nutshell. Three significant relationships shaped Jewish identity throughout history: the relationship with God, the relationship with the non-Jewish world, and the relationship between Jews and themselves. The nature of those relationships underwent a dramatic change within a short period.

The intimate relationship that Jews had with God became more distant. Granted, the Jews still boast of making monotheism the dominant religious fashion across the globe.[20] They still pride themselves on their teachings, which made God not only the one God, but also a special God, distinct from the physical world. They still believe they are the ones who removed God from the ancient, pagan world (idolatry was and still is the inverse of Judaism, considered pure evil).[21] However, as time passed, an increasing number of Jews no longer felt a need to have the traditional God in their lives. For many of them, the monotheistic message, with God as its focal point and the Commandments and way of life ascribed to Him, aren't as meaningful as they used to be. And sometimes, they aren't meaningful at all.

The Jews' relationship with the rest of the world—with the non-Jews—has also changed. For over 1,500 years, Jews were accustomed to being a foreign and distinct minority among the non-Jews, whether by choice or by force. A group at the mercy of others. But not anymore. Roughly half of the Jewish people now live in countries which (at least officially and legally) profess blessed indifference to the Jews' ancestry and religion and have granted them equal rights. Every individual has the right to live according to his beliefs or lack thereof. The other half of the Jewish people comprise the majority in a Jewish state which possesses organized and formal political, military, and economic power. The Jews make the rules and are no longer the passive players for whom the rules are made.

As a result of these developments and new circumstances, the relationship between the Jews and their own has also shifted. Those who live as equal citizens in different countries need to formulate a revised definition of the scope and substance of their ties with and commitment to Jews who live in other places. Those who live in Israel have to define their responsibility for the fate of other Jews who have chosen not to settle there. All are partners (or must explicitly choose not to be partners) in shaping a Jewish national home.[22] All are partners (or must expressly choose not to be partners) in reinterpreting the meaning of Jewishness at the crossroads where it now stands.

The philosopher Yitzhak Julius Guttmann witnessed the same Jewish world that Freud did.[23] He and many of his distinguished colleagues and students—including Gershom Scholem, Martin Buber, Abraham Joshua Heschel, Mordecai Kaplan, and others—attempted to understand the nature of Judaism in an era of modernization, enlightenment, science, and secularization.[24] Guttmann believed that all of these stripped the Jews of "Judaism's foundation of foundations."[25] In the Middle Ages, "one undisputed thing" constituted such a foundation, "and that was the belief in the divine origin of the Torah in the traditional sense." Jews believed that both the written and the oral Torah literally came from the mouth of God and that belief was the "common foundation underlying every discourse dealing with the essence of Judaism."

That diminished belief—and it has undoubtedly been depleted in the last few centuries—posed a difficult challenge to the Jews because if that foundation of foundations is missing, then what remains of Judaism?[26]

The ninth-century masterpiece, *The Book of Beliefs and Opinions,* written by Rabbi Saadia Gaon ("Rasag"), is the first treatise that can be called a book on Jewish philosophy.[27] He maintains that "our nation, the Children of Israel, is a nation only by virtue of its teachings." Those concise words encapsulate some of the fundamental dilemmas that modern-day Jews face.[28] On the one hand, the Children of Israel are a nation, perhaps what is now commonly called a people. On the other hand, they are a nation whose existence is contingent on a worldview, their "teachings," as Rasag puts it. Thus, at least according to a literal reading, a nation exists only if it is in possession of teachings.[29]

And what do those teachings stipulate? Rasag was among the first who tried to systematically formulate the essence of Judaism, which resulted in ten "principles of faith."[30, 31] Two centuries later, Maimonides increased their number to thirteen principles of faith, which are recited every morning in the *Shacharit* prayers. The principles relate to the existence of God, the unity of God, and the incorporeality of God, and they also touch on what was mentioned by Professor Guttmann: the divine origin of the Torah.[32] Whoever accepts those principles, Maimonides maintained, is "considered part of the Jewish people."[33] But what about those who don't embrace many of those principles, namely, what about the majority of Jews today?

An interim conclusion suggests there are two options:

Either Judaism is inflexible and immutable, founded on a firm ideological and conceptual doctrine, even though most people who consider themselves Jews no longer subscribe to it (because they don't accept the "principles").

Or that Judaism is not static, but flexible, and can be modified. If that's the case, then it's worth trying to redefine it in a manner consistent with the beliefs and opinions of Jews today (in other words, adapt Judaism to Jews).

What is Judaism?

It's quite a new brand, as Amos Oz and Fania Oz-Salzberger maintain in their book *Jews and Words*. It's a current substitute for what used to be "the People of Israel" and "Torah" and "Commandments." A substitute that "sounds scientific and dignified."[34]

It's no doubt elusive and subject to interpretation and debate. It's "the mystery of Israel," as the philosopher Emmanuel Levinas put it.[35] It is a mystery that can't be solved in a short chapter of a short book, but all the same, we'll suggest some of the many possibilities.

What is Judaism?

It's a question that could be answered from the outside: Namely, it's how non-Jews perceived and defined Jews and Judaism.[36] It wasn't always a flattering definition. The father of Marxism, Karl Marx, believed that Judaism is not only a religion but also "an attitude of spiritual slavery."[37] The British historian Arnold Toynbee described Judaism as a "fossil," an expendable remnant from the Middle Ages.[38] Adolf Hitler believed that Judaism perverted human nature and evicted man from the Garden of Eden, thereby imposing a needless law of good and bad on him.[39]

What is Judaism?

It's a question that could be answered from the inside: Namely, it's how the Jews themselves grasped and defined their Judaism. According to the Kabbalah scholar Gershom Scholem, Judaism is what every generation of Jews "chooses from the past, subtracts from and adds to, and redefines as the essence of Judaism as perceived by that generation."[40] In one of the biographies about the celebrated Jewish historian Heinrich Graetz, there's a nice story that describes a meeting between Graetz, still a young man, with another distinguished Jew of his period and a pioneer of the Jewish Studies movement, Leopold Zunz, in Berlin. [41, 42, 43]

Zunz wasn't especially cordial. When he heard about Graetz's intention to write a history of the Jews, he asked with scorn, "Another history of the Jews?"—as if there was no need for it. But Graetz wasn't intimidated. "But of course," he gladly replied. "But this time, it will be a Jewish history." In other words, it is not a history written by others who are critical and hostile, but Jewish history written from the perspective of a Jew.

Graetz chose to be a historian because he believed that theology and philosophy could only provide "partial and random" answers regarding the nature of Judaism.[44] Only from history can we learn the truth about the nature of Judaism.[45] As he saw it, what counts is what the Jews did, and not what they were supposed to do or what they were supposed to believe in.[46]

In any case, Graetz and the historians who followed him began writing a different kind of Jewish history, a history that is no longer subject to the old agenda and the rigid rules of the Jewish religion. They began writing history as they thought it should be written and began debating it as they thought it should be debated.

Jews never had a problem when it came to debate: Historians who came after Graetz, Simon Dubnow's contemporaries, maintained that their predecessors wrote history that was too intellectual and didn't place enough emphasis on the communal aspect of Jewish life. And the ones that came after them, including Salo Baron, claimed that their predecessors wrote a history that was too gloomy as it was comprised entirely of a chain of tragedies.[47] Zionist historians believed that Baron and those like him were unable to write a proper history because they were too busy trying to ingratiate themselves with their non-Jewish surroundings.[48] Post-Zionist historians argued that the Zionists were incapable of writing an adequate history because they were only interested in justifying the narrative, which claimed that the establishment of the State of Israel is the "height of the Jewish people's achievements."[49]

Nonetheless, after reading the expansive works of all these historians, who bicker with each other over many matters, one can glean a theme that sustained "the nation's continuity and solidarity even when its national and social frameworks were compromised."[50] That theme enabled the Jews to overcome the obstacles on their path and impelled them to preserve their culture in a foreign and often hostile environment. That theme joins the people and their faith.[51] Its essence: there's a covenant that God and the people of Israel share.[52] More precisely, a single God chose a single people and entered into a special covenant with them.[53]

The covenant isn't something that can be proven. It could very well be a "delusion, or at the very least an exaggeration," according to Arthur Hertzberg.[54] But it's difficult to argue with the fact that the covenant has existed in the minds of Jews for thousands of years. It's evident in the writings of rabbis, thinkers, religious scholars, and historians trying to decipher the essence of Judaism. And it's evident in the actions of Jews and in the way they organized themselves in covenant communities throughout the generations.[55]

Rabbi Joseph Soloveitchik called that covenant a "covenant of destiny" and distinguished between it and the parallel concept he coined, "a covenant of fate."[56] Even in Egypt, the Israelites shared a fate, but the Sinaitic covenant made them a special people. They are a people who have a religious covenant with God, and also a political covenant that binds them as a group. The two covenants combined distinguish the Jewish people as a unit who are not "a simple political or racial entity, but to an eminent degree, a spiritual people," as the historian Dubnow explained.[57]

The covenant is one of a religion and of a people. If it is a recurring theme in the consciousness of Jews throughout the generations, it embodies a decision to continue aspiring together to achieve an objective that will be defined through an ongoing dialogue. Perhaps some sort of "redemption"—of the individual, or the people, or of all mankind—the nature of which is, of course, disputed (we'll touch on this in the epilogue).[58]

But is the "covenant" itself the essence of Judaism?

The covenant is a concept, an idea. But perhaps Judaism isn't primarily an idea nor an ideological blueprint suspended in space.[59] After all, as history knows it, Judaism is not a theology or philosophical theory but rather a framework that envelops the fabric of human life. Judaism is what the Jews do: the lives of individuals and the life of a community, sustenance and clothing, holidays and festivals, behavioral norms in times of joy and sorrow. As we mentioned above, the latter is why the historian Graetz chose history: Only by documenting the lives of Jews can you explain what Judaism is. There is no "Judaism" in and of itself. There are only "Jews," and what they understand and do in "every generation" is "Judaism."

But documenting the lives of Jews also creates a problem because their lives change frequently: they're with or without statehood, with or without a Temple, with or without a prophecy, with or without a Sanhedrin, gathered or dispersed, in Israel or in foreign lands, in moments of prosperity or periods of persecution, with the women in the background or demanding full partnership. If each possible way of life articulates "Judaism," then no single way of life articulates "Judaism." On the other hand, if just one way of life out of all of them is "Judaism"—for instance, if only those Jews who observe the complete set of Commandments are deserving of the title "Judaism"—then the majority of Jews nowadays are not partners to "Judaism."[60]

So, we return to the concept of the covenant.

The covenant is an idea that's been incorporated into daily life. It's a notion that facilitates a sense of continuity. The world changes, the Jews adapt to needs and circumstances, but the covenant gets passed on.

The covenant dictates limits that circumscribe the space within which change can occur in the Jewish world, including its scope and substance. That was the case during the period of Exile that followed the destruction of the First Temple, the long Exile that came after the destruction of the Second Temple, the golden ages in Babylonia, Spain, and Turkey, and also during the various low points. It's clear that "the Judaism in Maimonides's time was as different from the Judaism in Ezra's days as Maimonides's world was different from Ezra's," wrote Rabbi Mordecai Kaplan, one of the most critical and progressive thinkers among America's Jews in the twentieth century.[61] In other words, there is little similarity between the way of life in the Marrakesh ghetto—the *mellah*—in the fifteenth century, and that of a farmer tending his vineyards in Samaria in the days of the united kingdom of David and Solomon in 1,000 BCE.[62]

Nevertheless—and even though 2,500 years separate the two kinds of Jews—the later Jew can easily identify himself as a direct descendant, both biologically and culturally, of the earlier one. Both viewed themselves as partners in the same covenant.[63]

Can Jews working in high-tech in Ra'anana, Israel, or in San Francisco in the twenty-first century also view themselves as successors of that covenant? It's not always simple. The covenant established that a Jew has two bonds—one with other Jews (because the covenant is a collective matter) and one with God (who cements the group together). But many Jews today don't necessarily feel comfortable with those bonds. Some are uncomfortable with the bond with other Jews because historical circumstances—emancipation, nationalism, equality—joined them with the modern-day country and society they live in. Some find it hard to rely on God because they no longer accept the literal meaning of the "divine origin of the Torah," and they don't believe in God and His Commandments. They cannot accept God's choice as the foundation of the Covenant.

Jews are looking for ways to resolve this uneasiness: every Jew and his or her solution.

One relatively simple solution is to disengage from the Jewish journey. Quite a few Jews across the globe have decided to do so, by action or omission, and choose to assimilate and vanish. They're no longer obligated to an ancient covenant with an entity they don't believe in. Some Jews in Israel are also looking to do the same by advancing "Israeliness" and civic normality, which are free of the yoke of Jewish culture.[64]

But those who are interested in the Jewish story should be looking at the Jews who insist on sustaining that thing called Judaism in a format tailored to modern times. Those interested in the Jewish story have reason to be optimistic about the prospects of sustaining that thing called "Judaism" in a format tailored to modern times. Judaism managed to adapt to different kinds of life circumstances in the past, and there's no reason it won't adapt now as well.

How did Judaism adapt? There's an abundance of options and ways.

Two significant movements in contemporary Judaism sought to make it more current by emphasizing the religious foundation at the expense of the national foundation. That's what Orthodox Judaism did, whose response to modernization was to draft new norms that imposed rabbinic authority on Jews in order to entrench rigid traditions and prevent disengagement from a way of life that dictated fulfilling the Commandments.[65] And that's what Reform Judaism did, which sought to establish a place of worship devoid—or nearly devoid—of a national foundation.[66] Other important movements in contemporary Judaism—of which political Zionism is a prominent example—wanted to modernize and repair Judaism through a reverse emphasis on its national foundation at the expense of the religious one.[67] Many Zionist leaders claimed to emancipate the Jews not only from the rule of non-Jews but also from the tyranny of Jewish religious tradition.

Those and other movements challenge Jews with an innovative agenda that is supposed to be compatible with the current reality. Nowadays, only a handful of them still hope to achieve a dramatic change: to strip Judaism entirely of its religious or national component. Most are looking for more moderate adjustments, the gist of which usually entails a transition from a compound made up of a people and its religion to a compound that can envelop all Jews. It's no longer a covenant between the people and God, but between the people and the ideas and ideals that are the essence of its tradition and culture (and whoever wants to continue believing in God; all the better).

The shift of the covenant from a faith-based partnership to a cultural partnership was facilitated by historians, starting with Graetz, who revolutionized the way the reality was perceived. By writing Jewish history, they not only broadened the knowledge about Jews but also altered how Jews looked at themselves. When Jewish history began to be rewritten, "a new type of Jew" emerged. The place of the ritual Jew, who identified with his traditions using religious means, was replaced by a Jew who formulates his identity "on the basis of the historical experience of the nation," the historical Jew.[68] And in the eyes of the latter Jew, the bond between Jews is no longer formed by a covenant mediated by God. Mostly, it's created by the foundation molded by a shared past.

Rabbi Mordecai Kaplan was the most prominent among Jewish thinkers to adapt to this shift in the way Judaism was perceived: "The life of a nation," he wrote, "is a communal form of life whose unity rests, more than anything else, on culture or civilization."[69] He rejected the view that underscores the religious foundations of Judaism because it doesn't enable the Jews to survive the challenges of the modern age. He also rejected a national view stripped of any religious substance because it doesn't adequately acknowledge the critical importance of religion for the existence of culture. Kaplan's Jewish civilization is both national and religious.[70] But it's not national in the classic Zionist sense, because he objected to the Jews undergoing a process of normalization in their own country. And it's not religious according to the Orthodox or Reform tenets, because he objected to viewing Judaism primarily as a religion and wanted Jews to have a religious foundation that doesn't entail belief in an immaterial divine.[71] In other words, he strived for Jewish religiosity that doesn't necessarily include God. (There is a joke about the Jew whose son asks him about the Holy Trinity—the Father, the Son, and the Holy Spirit—and the father replies: "My son, the God we don't believe in is the only one.)

Like Kaplan, Ahad Ha'am (Asher Ginsberg) stood out among the Jewish thinkers who sought to adapt their understanding of Judaism to the changing times. He, too, was a Jew of nationality and culture.[72] Being inordinately secular, his renunciation of the fulfillment of the Commandments—which he felt was a personal decision that doesn't pertain to the collective—can be misleading: Ahad Ha'am drew a lot from the conservative version of the religious and spiritual tradition, and his prerequisites for a Jewish existence were quite demanding.[73] He believed that a Jewish state devoid of a suitable "national culture"—as he wrote in his important essay *The Jewish State and the Jewish Problem*—"will be the deadly drug of our people and lower its spirit to ashes."[74]

Ahad Ha'am advocated for an ethical Jewish state whose morality rests on the sources of Judaism.[75] In a blistering critique he wrote about a play by Zionist leader Max Nordau called *Doctor Kohn*; Ahad Ha'am vividly renounces Jewish nationalism that is detached from what he identified as Jewish ethics.[76]

The hero of the play agrees to fight a duel against an antisemite who insults the Jewish people. He accepts the challenge so no one will think that "Jews are cowardly, who hear their dishonor but don't respond with a dagger and blood!" The playwright, Nordau, deemed this a display of Jewish heroism. Ahad Ha'am disapproved because he considered it a form of Gentile hooliganism. The willingness to fight a duel, the willingness to shed blood due to an insult to one's "honor" (the quotation marks appear in the original, in Ahad Ha'am's critique), is contrary "not only to the commandments of the religion but also to the very moral sentiment in our hearts," he wrote.

According to Ahad Ha'am, "moral sentiment" is the essence of Judaism.[77] And he's not the only contemporary Jewish thinker who equated "Judaism" with some sort of "morality." In the eyes of many Jews, Jewish morality is the essence of Judaism.

Jews can be bonded by a chain of concepts that can be used by anyone reflecting on the nature of contemporary Judaism. It's a long chain of values, customs, language, texts, dates, and historical memory. It's a chain that some Jews call "culture," others call "peoplehood," and some even go so far as to call "civilization."[78] All these names are rather vague and can be interpreted however one likes.

Moshe Halbertal classified Jews and their beliefs into three categories or three types found in the modern Jewish age,[79] each representing a different response to the question of what Judaism is.

One type is the "cosmopolitan" Jew. He believes that morality is the essence of Judaism. Perfected by experience, it's a set of values (which we'll discuss in a later chapter) that Judaism developed and imparted to the world. Many Jews today, renowned philosophers and ordinary Jews alike, are "cosmopolitan." They set Jewish priorities, with leading an "ethical life" and working for "justice" and "equality" at the top of the list.[80, 81]

The second type is the "traditional" Jew. Although there are strong indications of a crisis of faith among some Jews, religion and faith are still with us, and the traditional type of Jew considers them the core of Judaism. Many Jews feel a strong bond with the Jewish religion, including the divine origin of the Torah in one form or another. Most Jews living in Israel will answer in the affirmative when asked if the "Jewish people are the chosen people among all the nations." The majority of them believe that "God gave the Land of Israel to the Jews," and most maintain that "God exists."[82] Around a quarter of the Jews living in the United States believe in God "as described in the Bible," and one in ten described Judaism as mostly a religion.[83]

The third type is the "national" Jew. After all, despite the abundance of hardships, the bond of a nation, or a people, is still with us. The most significant undertaking of the Jews in the last century underscored their existence as a national entity. The majority of Jews who are full partners to that undertaking, Israeli Jews, consider themselves part of a greater Jewish universe.[84] Additionally, most Jews who observe that national undertaking from a distance in the Diaspora—and demonstrate active involvement in it to one degree or another—acknowledge its centrality to all Jews and feel connected to it.[85]

Against the backdrop of these three types, one can suggest the following response to the question of what Judaism is today:

Judaism today is still a covenant. It's a covenant between several types of Jews, each of whom interprets the essence of Judaism in his own way; a covenant between several types of Jews who are prepared to continue debating what Judaism is and view themselves as the subjects of that discussion.

And we'll now ask: But which "type" should even be called a Jew?

What Is Judaism: A Few Options

1) Primarily a **religion** (more suitable to Jewish life in the Diaspora)

   and/or

   Primarily a **nationality** (more suitable to statehood in Israel)

2) A set of **ideas** (there is "Judaism" and there are "Jews")

   and/or

   A **way of life** (Judaism is what Jews do)

3) A covenant founded on a **bond with God** (faith, observance of the Commandments)

   and/or

   A covenant founded on a **historical bond** (tradition, language, peoplehood, ethics)

Question 2:

Who's a Jew?

The life of a Jew requires focus and direction, and cannot be carried out offhandedly. One who thinks that one can live as a Jew in a lackadaisical manner has never tasted Judaism.
(Abraham Joshua Heschel)[86]

Meet Hannah and David, from New York.

This is their story: She's the daughter of a Jewish father and a Protestant mother. She grew up in a Reform Jewish community that was "nice and inclusive, even though everyone knew that my mother wasn't exactly Jewish." He's the son of an Episcopalian father and Catholic mother, who grew up "without any particular interest in God, perhaps because my parents didn't manage to agree on which direction to take." When he married Hannah, he agreed that their children would be Jewish. As time passed, he too became "kind of Jewish"—without rituals, without conversion. It just happened. And the children? "They'll decide on their own." They are, in fact, "Jewish," but without parental insistence on exclusivity. Also-Jews, but not only-Jews. Because there's a family and there are surroundings, and there's "a lot of beauty in every tradition," as Hannah says.[87]

Jews? Not Jews?

It depends on who's asking. It depends on "Jewish" for what purpose. It depends on who decides if anyone can even make such a decision. It's not easy to define what belonging means in a world of free choice.

Certain communities won't recognize any members of the above family as being Jewish. If there's no Jewish mother (or conversion), they are not Jews. That verdict is likely reached by communities that rely on the ancient tradition of matrilineal descent, whose origin and initial date of appearance are murky.[88] In the Bible, the father is the one who passes down Jewish status to his children. By the time of the Mishnah, it's the mother. The change occurred sometime in between. Maybe it was in the days of Ezra when foreign wives and their children were banished (it's unclear whether that decision was carried out).[89,90,91] Perhaps it was later, in the wake of the Bar Kokhba revolt, in response to the mass rape of Jewish women by Roman soldiers (one of several theories), which prompted the rabbis of the time to amend the law so the children born to those women would not be excluded from the Jewish people.

In retrospect, there are many ways to justify and explain why matrilineal descent was preferred and how it is consistent with the spirit of Judaism.[92] But other justifications, no less solid, could be provided to defend a different choice. And in fact, a different choice was made, which was also justified at length. It occurred toward the end of the twentieth century when the institutions of Reform Judaism decided to recognize the Jewish status of a child born to a Jewish father (in addition to matrilineal descent) due to the changing circumstances."[93, 94, 95]

It was a landmark event because, by making that decision, Reform Jews broke with ancient traditions and changed the face of the largest Jewish community in the world and, with it, the face of world Jewry.[96, 97] And they achieved that in two ways: by redefining the accepted norm of who is a Jew; and, no less important, by shattering the illusion that there's even somebody who can decide for all Jews who a Jew is.

A few generations following the aforementioned decision, in the middle of the second decade of the twenty-first century, American Jewry reportedly reached a watershed moment: One out of every two young Jews in the United States has only one Jewish parent. When their time comes, most of them will also marry non-Jewish partners.[98] That's already the case among most Jews in America. Some of the children born to those couples will be Jewish, but not according to the accepted definitions from the past, and they too will continue marrying non-Jews, and so on and so forth.

Will all those children be considered Jews by other Jews?

Whoever refuses to regard them as Jews will bear a heavy responsibility for causing a schism in the Jewish people.[99] Jewish history is not unfamiliar with such schisms, when in the days of the Mishnah, Jews were forbidden from marrying Samaritans, or when marriages between Jews and Karaites were prohibited in later periods.[100]

Whoever refuses to regard so many Jews as Jews will risk not only sectarianism but also, and perhaps primarily, they will risk becoming irrelevant. Who authorized anyone to exclude anyone from the Jewish people? Can a minority exclude the majority? Can a minority decide who's a Jew? Isn't the person doing the excluding liable to find himself excluded?

The possibility of a split hovers over this chapter, and it's not something inconceivable. The core of the question of who's a Jew is who makes that decision. Does the law determine what the people should look like, or do the people determine what the law should look like? And if it's the law that decides, who makes the law? (It could, after all, be the people.) And if the people are the ones who decide—who are the people—only those who meet the definitions of the law?

When looking to answer these questions, one could continue clinging to the story about the revolution in the Reform movement, regarding which there's also no consensus as to who decided, for whom, and why. Perhaps it was a necessary ideological decision that rested, among other things, on a basic worldview that espouses gender equality (explaining why the mother shouldn't have preference over the father).[101] But, surely, one can also maintain that it was an adaptation of the ideology to the reality of life. In other words, through its actions (by marrying non-Jews), the public has dictated a new worldview. American society changed and emphasized every person's right to "choose the spiritual path he finds meaningful and is comfortable with."[102] And when American society changed, so did American Jews—because the Jews in America followed America's cue. It was no longer acceptable to insist that every non-Jewish partner undergo conversion. The rate of intermarriages rose. And under those circumstances, the decision to adopt patrilineal descent was simply well-timed. It didn't stem from ideology but from the Jews' need to facilitate the way of life they had already chosen.

We asked, who decides who's a Jew?

It's a delicate and complicated question, the answer to which can be found between two extremes.[103] Some believe that "Jewishness" is, first and foremost, a personal matter that everyone determines on their own. Thus, a person's Jewishness is primarily determined by professing his belonging to the Jewish people. It's a choice made by the individual. That viewpoint receives inspiration from the beautiful story about Ruth the Moabite, who at a decisive moment declared: "Your people shall be my people, and your God my God." Without any religious court, without any ritual immersion, and without any ceremony.

The other extreme can generally be called *halakhic,* and those who subscribe to it prefer certain rules and clear definitions that facilitate an examination of who is and who isn't, of who's in and who's out. Were you born to a Jewish mother? Then you're Jewish. Did you convert through the proper rabbinic channels? Then you're Jewish. And what about Ruth? There's no problem with Ruth because, based on the talmudic tradition that interpreted the biblical narrative, Ruth underwent a proper conversion. According to one commentary, she did it when traveling with Naomi; according to another, she converted "when still a child."[104]

So, in a nutshell, here's the key to understanding most of the debates over the question of who's a Jew: Imagine the Jewish people as a closed, defined group. Imagine a fence that surrounds them with a gate. Imagine that the Jewish people used to be such a group that the fence encircling them utterly separated them from the rest of the world. Whoever was born behind the fence was Jewish. Whoever wanted to come in from the outside had to pass through the gate. There were agreed-upon criteria that determined who could pass through the gate (the conversion process), and guards (the authority that stipulates the way to convert) were positioned at the gate.

What happened to that gate is what happened to the question of who's a Jew. There was once a fence that had only one gate. But then, other gates were built—namely, there was no longer just one form of conversion that everyone accepted, but rather a number of conversion options (Orthodox, Reform, lenient, strict, Israeli, diasporic). Whoever didn't get a ticket to enter through one gate could buy a ticket to another at a different price. And suddenly, the group wasn't exactly a group anymore, because it included people who came in through different gates with differently priced tickets. And suddenly, the fence wasn't exactly a fence anymore. And if it's not really a fence, then why is one even needed?

So, who's a Jew today? Certainly not only those who were once considered Jews. In the absence of a fence and a gate, interesting things are happening that didn't occur in the past. And they're happening for the most part among Jews who lead a Western way of life, who live in a Western society that blurs ethnic and religious boundaries between different groups in the population. And they're happening primarily among those who not only ask who decides who's a Jew, but who also ask whether someone even needs to decide who's a Jew.

In a comprehensive study of New York Jews conducted in 2012, some Jews were counted based solely on their "personal choice"—Jews who don't have a Jewish parent and didn't convert.[105] They are Jews who decided on their own that they're Jewish. That same study also included quite a few "partially Jewish" Jews—namely, those who identify as Jews, but not exclusively.[106] Similar to the self-defined Jews, the partially Jewish are a new category in Judaism, stemming from the large number of interfaith families that want their children to "celebrate both religions," both of the father as well as the mother.[107]

Not all Jews will agree that the "partially Jewish" are in fact Jews. Nor do all researchers of Judaism agree on that. Some researchers have chosen not to count those Jews who consider themselves Jewish but don't have Jewish parents, weren't raised as Jews, and weren't converted.[108,109] These more conservative researchers created a new and separate category for them: people with a "Jewish affinity."[110]

The debates over the question of what Judaism is (see the previous chapter) engender competing answers to the question of who is a Jew. That being the case, even in Israel—which is a political entity that requires clear definitions for different needs—there are at least two definitions of Jews: according to the Ministry of Interior, a Jew is one thing (most conversions count). According to the Chief Rabbinate—which is also a government agency—a Jew is something else (only Orthodox conversions count).[111]

It's a natural and rather expected situation, given the lack of consensus between the different Jewish communities over who is a Jew and who decides who is a Jew. In the past, rabbis and religious leaders made that decision. But many Jews no longer consider them a fitting authority. Yossi Beilin, a former Israeli cabinet minister, once asked: "Why does a non-Jew, who doesn't believe in God, have to go to a rabbi to become a Jew who doesn't believe in God?" Even believers nowadays are not like what they used to be. They may believe, but don't deduce uniform rules of behavior from their faith. They may believe, but don't necessarily think that Judaism is a religious matter, and certainly not a matter of a religious lifestyle.[112] As noted above, some prefer a vaguer definition that views Judaism as a matter of "ancestry and culture."[113]

If Judaism is "ancestry and culture" and not a religion, it's easy to understand those who wish to define their belonging to Judaism not according to rules set by religious leaders, as was done in the past, but according to a new foundation.

Proposals of that nature, some more detailed and others less, emerge from time to time regarding the conversion process. For example, Professor Steven Cohen and Rabbi Kerry Olitzky called for instituting "Jewish Cultural Affirmation."[114] The researcher, Rabbi Dov Maimon, suggested a similar option which, as he sees it, has a dual advantage: it would exempt rabbis from deceiving themselves when they compel would-be Jews to undergo religious conversion when it's clear they don't want to observe the Commandments, and it would also exempt those who wish to become Jews, but not in the religious sense, from the need to feign interest in the Torah and the Commandments.[115] Maimon proposed that the Jewish Agency confer Jewish certification. The researcher Regev Ben David formulated an idea he called "intercom"—namely, different models of conversion that bring Jews into the same "condominium" (the Jewish people) in a variety of ways, but only after agreeing that the distinctiveness of each "apartment" within the building will be maintained.[116]

Different Jewish denominations are distinct, just like the ideological sects that comprise them. And apart from the denominations, there are Jews who don't belong to any of them or aren't believers. And there are Jews who consider themselves Jewish, but "not by religion," or identify with "secular Jewish culture," or view themselves as members of a people that isn't necessarily religious.[117,118] And there's also a trait that divides the Jewish people into two camps nearly equal in size, split between one type of framework of Jews who live in Jewish communities and a different framework of Jews who live in a Jewish State.

From the outset, we can see an unbridgeable gap between Israel and Diaspora Jews in all that concerns the question of who is a Jew. Israel needs a simple and precise definition that can be incorporated into laws and political arrangements. Jews in the Diaspora, on the other hand, are able—and many also want—to cope with gray areas or those devoid of any definition at all.[119] That disparity can potentially make the two groups grow apart and even lead to a rift: if the Jews in Israel insist on defining Jewish as one thing while Jews around the world define Jewish as being something else, the Jewish people will become two peoples.[120]

Almost seventy years have elapsed since the State of Israel's first prime minister, David Ben-Gurion, initiated the most important survey conducted in the modern period, which dealt with the question of who is a Jew—the survey of surveys of the Jewish people.[121,122] It's worth taking another look at it because some of the circumstances that engendered it are still valid.

The year: 1958. The issue on the agenda: How should the children of a new immigrant couple, with a Jewish father and a non-Jewish mother, be registered in the religion and nationality sections of the Population Registry?[123]

The parents wanted to register their children as Jews. The Ministry of Interior had no objection to that. The directives issued by the then–Minister of Interior, Israel Bar-Yehuda, a member of the Ahdut Ha'avoda party, sanctioned the registration. Relying on an opinion obtained from Attorney General Haim Cohn (who later became the deputy president of the Supreme Court), Bar-Yehuda stipulated that a Jew is any person who chooses in good faith to call himself a Jew—namely, self-determination.[124]

The religious parties objected to that decision. The ministers from the National Religious Party resigned from the government and declared that, "for us, the unity of the Jewish people and nation is a sacred principle."[125] Minister Bar-Yehuda wanted to enable each individual to decide "in good faith" whether he is a Jew. The National Religious Party ministers sought to safeguard the principle that it's not the individual, but the authorities who decide.

The debate became even more heated. Most objectors were religious and protested: Who authorized the minister of interior to change a thousands-year-old tradition? The supporters, most of whom were non-observant, responded: Why should a secular nation-state give rabbis the keys to the front gate of the Jewish people?[126]

A fundamental question was put to the test, which has not yet been resolved: Does the establishment of the Jewish state alter the condition of the Jewish people in a way that can justify a sweeping revolution in how a person's Jewishness is defined? Yitzhak Ben-Aharon, a member of Ahdut Ha'avoda, replied in the affirmative: "In Israel, an Israeli nation is evolving, whose collective hallmark is not the religious affiliation." A member of Knesset, Menachem Begin, from Herut, (and later the PM), disagreed with him and endorsed the traditional stance: "We don't have the right to determine who's a Jew…our forefathers determined who's a Jew."[127]

The debate dealt with ideas and principles, but the political crisis was very concrete, and the government had to make the call. It made three decisions: 1. The disputed directives were revoked. 2. Only a person who does not profess "any other religion" will be allowed to register as a Jew. 3. An opinion would be sought from "Jewish wisemen" regarding the overall question of who is a Jew. A letter detailing the essence of the issue, signed by Ben-Gurion, was in fact sent to about fifty scholars and rabbis, most of whom accepted the challenge.

The scholars identified with religious Orthodox Judaism—about half of the respondents—replied in a way expected of them.[128] They included Chief Rabbi Shlomo Goren and Rabbi Yitzhak Halevi Herzog, as well as the Nobel Prize–winning novelist S. Y. Agnon, who wrote the following to Ben-Gurion: "I concur with the sages of Israel, who concur with and are faithful to the Torah, as it was interpreted by our sages of blessed memory and stated in the *Shulchan Aruch.* And I have nothing to add to their statements or to subtract from them at all." The majority of the respondents (thirty-five) agreed that the traditional halakhic definition also suits the reality in Israel.

In his reply, Moshe Maisels, the editor and translator, described in harsh words the challenge that the Jewish state poses for the path of the Jewish people: "Like any other creation, something made out of nothing involves danger...one can never clearly know what its nature is...this passing generation, the father of the new entity...must multiply the Jewish 'is' in Israel to minimize the danger in the evolvement of something out of nothing."[129] The State of Israel is too young to assess its impact on the Jewish world. So, it's too early to change the rules because of Israel. The philosopher Samuel Hugo Bergmann expressed a similar sentiment in his letter: "The State of Israel is founded on premises that the halakha cannot accept," he wrote. In Israel, the elected officials and the bureaucrats decide, whereas in Jewish law, the rabbis decide. "We cannot blur this tragic contradiction and must wait for history's judgment, which will demonstrate if the people of Israel want to remain faithful to their religious foundation or be a nation like all nations."

The people of Israel? But who exactly are those "people of Israel" who may prefer it this way or that way? Who exactly are the Jewish people who are waiting for history's judgment? And now, close to eighty years after the establishment of Israel, is it possible to determine which judgment was pronounced?

Private Yevgeny Tolochko is buried in the military cemetery on Jerusalem's Mount Herzl, Section A, Lot 23, Row 1, Grave No. 2. He died in February 2013, while still in basic training.[130] Two months later, when it came time for Israel's Independence Day celebrations, Tolochko was the Israel Defense Forces (IDF)'s most recent casualty—which, in keeping with tradition, meant that the chief of staff would visit his grave and place a flag on it.

But the chief of staff, Lieutenant General Benny Gantz, placed a flag on the grave of another soldier in that cemetery. It was the grave of Shlomo "Moni" Nitzani, who died in October of the previous year. Nitzani had been awarded a medal of honor for his bravery and sacrifice during the 1957 Sinai Campaign and was also the recipient of a distinguished service medal for "his leadership skills, steadfastness, courage and presence of mind" in the southern front during the 1973 Yom Kippur War.

Nitzani was a lieutenant colonel and a hero. Tolochko was just a simple soldier. Furthermore, Nitzani was Jewish, whereas Tolochko's status was unclear.

Because he wasn't recognized as a Jew by the rabbis, Tolochko was buried in a lot reserved for non-Jews. This is a peculiar Israeli reality: the Law of Return permits the immigration, absorption, and citizenship of new immigrants like Tolochko. They are also called up for military service. The Law of Return treats them like Jews—but other protocols pertaining to Jews do not apply to them. They can't get married in Israel, because marriage between Jews is under the jurisdiction of the Rabbinate, and the rabbis won't allow it. And if those immigrants are killed in the line of duty, their burial in the same lots with Jews is a challenge for the Military Rabbinate.

Tolochko's case was not the first where Israel had to deal with this reality and try and come to terms with its significance. Twenty years earlier, there was the story of Lev Pesachov, a soldier with a Jewish father who was killed in Lebanon in 1993. The rabbis decided to bury Pesachov next to the fence in the cemetery, creating a public outrage, following which his body was moved to a more central location.

Was he a Jew? Was he a non-Jew?

In Pesachov's case, it was the public who decided, and decided in the affirmative: Pesachov was Jewish enough to be buried next to Jews. According to the philosopher Moshe Halbertal, the public campaign to relocate his grave "signifies just how deep the modern consciousness of solidarity is as a foundation in defining Jewish identity."[131] And he was right—but not entirely. It depends on the case, it depends on the soldier, and it depends on the public's reaction. The solidarity consciousness prevails sometimes, whereas a different consciousness, the historical-halakhic one, prevails on other occasions.[132]

The fact that Tolochko's grave was passed over did not go unnoticed. Sharp criticism was leveled at the army, and the chief of staff found himself in an awkward position.[133] He went to visit the family and explained that a mistake had been made, which he was not aware of. But after that, the IDF only added insult to injury: Starting the following year, the army promised instead of one flag on one grave, two flags would be placed on two graves—one for a Jew and one for a non-Jew.

Member of Knesset Elazar Stern, a retired IDF general, saw and seized the opportunity. Stern is known to be especially sensitive to issues concerning the conversion and status of soldiers who are not recognized as Jews.[134] Tolochko's case provoked him to announce his intention to introduce a bill that would require soldiers to be buried next to one another. "As I see it, it's unfair to separate soldiers who fight shoulder to shoulder after their deaths," he said. He also added—echoing Prof. Halbertal's contention—that, in his opinion, death in uniform was the "ultimate conversion." A soldier killed while defending the State of Israel is Jewish enough to be buried in a lot with other Jews."[135]

So, this, too, is a new way of defining who's a Jew: whoever fights as a Jew for the Jewish state. Or, more generally, whoever is a partner in the Jewish destiny.[136]

Stern threatened legislation but eventually made do with a compromise—soldiers would be buried in the same lots, but in different rows. He was comfortable with the compromise because it "reflects the complex profile of Israel's society" and its divided opinions. Some people view the sacrifice inherent in enlisting in the army as "ultimate conversion"—a modern gateway to the Jewish people. On the other hand, some still insist on the historic, halakhic gateway.

Echoes of this controversy can be found in the old letters sent by the scholars to Ben-Gurion. The jurist, Haim Cohn, wrote the following to the prime minister: "Matters of this nature should at this time be treated in the Land of Israel differently than in foreign countries.... Everyone here is presumed Jewish...."[137] A direct line connects Cohn, an avowed atheist, to the national-religious Stern. Both of them view the Israeli reality as having redrawn the boundaries of Jewish belonging. Both believe that living in Israel converts, and that the uniform converts.

A definition revised to meet the Israeli reality will be a dramatic turning point in the annals of the Jewish people, but not an unprecedented one.[138] There have been periods in Jewish history when Jewishness was more of a national matter than a religious one. However, Israel is home to less than half of the Jewish people. And as far as the other half is concerned, a "national" definition could be problematic.

Is Judaism a matter of faith (in the right God), or behavior (on Yom Kippur), or ancestry (Jewish parents), or ancient laws (a Jewish mother), or a shared Jewish destiny (serving in the IDF), or exclusivity (does not profess any other religion), or self-determination (I'm a Jew)? Maybe it was once clear who is Jewish, perhaps they used to be a homogenous group—but not anymore. Every definition changes how many Jews there are. Every definition redraws the boundaries of the community.

Who is a Jew?

In conclusion, there seem to be three possibilities: those who decide on their own that they are Jewish; whoever the Jews decide are Jewish; or a third option—which has gained popularity since the Holocaust—the non-Jews will decide for the Jews who is Jewish. The renowned British philosopher Isaiah Berlin raised that possibility in his letter to Ben-Gurion. As Berlin saw it, the question of who is a Jew should be guided by "the common sense criterion, according to which a Jew is someone who is taken to be a Jew by his neighbors, and particularly by his Gentile neighbors."[139,140]

WHO IS A JEW TODAY: SOME DISPUTED POSSIBILITIES

The Jewish people decides according to traditional criteria (parent, conversion):

A Jew is someone whose mother is Jewish or underwent Orthodox conversion (an intra-Orthodox debate also exists over the procedure).

A Jew is someone whose mother is Jewish or converted in an accepted manner (and different approaches exist—who is authorized to conduct the conversion, and how).

A Jew is someone who has a Jewish parent, who was raised as a Jew and declares that he is a Jew—or converted (the official position of the Reform movement).

The person himself decides (and the Jewish people accept it):

A Jew is someone who decides he is a Jew (and we accept him with open arms).

A Jew is someone who takes action for the greater Jewish good (and does not profess any other religion).

External circumstances dictate:

A Jew is someone who the non-Jewish world considers a Jew.

Question 3:

What Are Jewish Values?

"Love your neighbor as yourself," Rabbi Akiva says: This is a cardinal principle of the Torah. Ben Azzai says: "This is the book of the generations of Adam." That is an even greater principle.
(Jerusalem Talmud, Nedarim 9:4)[141]

The Jews are an argumentative people, and the Jewish God undoubtedly knows that. Abraham, the father of the nation, stood across from God and defiantly asked, "Would you obliterate the righteous along with the wicked?"[142] Moses, the greatest prophet, persuaded God not to destroy the Israelites.[143] The prophet Jeremiah fearlessly expressed his anger against God. And Gideon the Judge also behaved in an insolent manner.[144] But of all the confrontations between man and God, including the more and the less famous ones, the argument between King Saul and God on the eve of the battle against the Amalekites is particularly engaging. That argument does not appear in the biblical account of the events in the Book of Samuel.[145] It appears only in a later commentary in the Talmud.

The story of the battle is dramatic and so is its horrific outcome. It resulted in the annihilation of the Amalekites; it led to the tragic end of the Kingdom of Saul following the king's failure to complete the mission as dictated to him. Saul did not destroy the best of the Amalekites' sheep and cattle and spared King Agag's life.

The beginning of the story does not predict its end. Samuel the Prophet commands Saul to "go and smite Amalek." According to the text, Saul does as he is commanded: "And Saul came as far as the city of Amalek and set an ambush in the valley."

But this is precisely where the Talmud intervenes and describes the battle as a twisted affair from the start. The Talmud tells us that there was a bitter confrontation between Saul and God before the battle.[146] The words in the biblical passage—and in particular the Hebrew word *VaYarev* (that comes from the word *merivah,* which means an argument or fight), coupled with the mention of a valley—are suggestive of that confrontation. Saul argues with God and refers to a matter pertaining to a valley. And what is that matter pertaining to a valley? It's the biblical law of the "decapitated calf." If a person is found dead and no one knows who killed him, the elders from the closest town are required to go down to the nearest valley and hold a ceremony in which they accept responsibility for the murder and ask to be forgiven for not preventing it.[147] According to the Talmud, Saul is averse to obeying the command to slaughter the Amalekites.[148] How can it be, he complains to God, that owing to one unidentified victim, the blameless elders of the clan are dispatched to a rite of atonement—the "decapitated calf"—whereas he, King Saul, is expected to slaughter men, women, old people, children, and livestock indiscriminately?

Abraham raises a similar moral dilemma with God before the destruction of Sodom. God listens patiently and takes Abraham's position into consideration. When Moses makes an appeal—"turn from Your fierce anger"[149]—following God's decision to destroy the Israelites, God is quick to grant his request.[150]

But that doesn't happen in Saul's case. The king receives a sharp reprimand, and a humiliating rebuff: "And a voice [from heaven] was heard saying: do not be over-righteous."[151]

The first and obvious question in the context of the term "Jewish values" is one that any decent person is likely to ask himself when faced with the story of Saul: who decides what a Jewish value is—the Torah or one's conscience?[152] Depending on the period and the worldview, one can also phrase that question differently: who decides—God or man? The strict letter of Jewish law or evolving human ethics? An ideal that has become embedded in tradition or what Jews feel in a particular generation?[153]

One possible answer is that there are no such thing as Jewish values. Judaism only has the words of God as articulated in the Torah. Whoever accepts the Torah must abide by its teachings, and whoever embraces human values or ethics should act according to them. That argument is consistent with Professor Yeshayahu Leibowitz's doctrine, who posited that "morality is an atheistic category" and not a Jewish one.[154, 155] That doesn't mean a person can't choose to be moral.[156] It only means that Judaism doesn't require it. Every directive in Jewish texts that shows signs of being a moral directive—whether coming from the Torah, the Prophets, or the later literature dealing with ethics—has a single purpose: to guide the Jew toward fulfilling the Commandments.

Some other viewpoints resemble the one that Leibowitz subscribed to. We won't mention them all, but we will mention one as an example: the possibility that there are also Jewish values that coexist with the Torah, and at times one may think that what's written in the Torah contradicts what those Jewish values embody. According to that viewpoint, the contradiction is imagined—the problem lies in man's lack of understanding and not in any actual clash between the Torah and other Jewish values.[157] Like with Leibowitz, that viewpoint is based on a rule from which there's no deviating: regardless of what its content looks like, the Torah always has the final say. The Torah may give human beings some leeway to make choices, but it also sets a clear direction that indicates who makes the right choice—it's the "person who lives in fear of God and follows His path."[158]

If Jewish values are the ones which the Torah commands adherence to, then they're obvious: keeping the Sabbath is a value, caring for the frail is a value, studying Torah is a value, and returning a lost item to its owner is a value. Preserving the sanctity of life is a value.[159] Destroying Amalek, men and women, the young and old, is also a value.[160]

And there's no contradiction between all those values because they all derive from the same source: God and the Torah. So when Saul questions the command he received, he's not displaying ethical-moral fortitude but rather ethical-moral confusion. It must have slipped his mind that morality is what God says it is. Saul shouldn't have taken an example from Abraham and Sodom, but from Abraham and the sacrifice of Isaac—from the

Abraham who doesn't waver when he receives the command that is the hardest for the human conscience to digest—and obeys without argument.[161]

But there is, of course, another possibility: that there are Jewish values, and they occasionally clash with what's written in traditional Jewish texts.[162] Those values were acquired in the course of a Jewish history replete with events and, for that reason, also replete with moral lessons. Due to their life circumstances, Jews developed a set of feelers that are sensitive to injustice. They developed a system of mutual responsibility. They developed a special ability to identify evil and malice. They developed increased empathy toward the weak, the vulnerable, the persecuted, and the excluded. When there are signs that this set of values is inconsistent with ancient Jewish tradition, Jews have to decide how to deal with them.[163]

That's what happened to the philosopher Samuel Hugo Bergmann, who had a hard time with Saul's story and the conclusion arising from it. As a Jewish humanist, Bergmann was unable to agree with the command to destroy Amalek. That led him to write that "the principle has to be" that "wherever the holy text is at odds with my moral sensibilities, I must sacrifice the text and not my intellect or my sensibility." Bergmann favors an Abrahamic Sodom-style response or a Saul Amalek-style response whenever there's a clash between what the Torah dictates and what our conscience dictates.[164] In the contemporary Jewish world, many can relate to such a response (which in its purest form is an appeal to completely abandon "Jewish values" because they are no longer valid).[165] The lessons of the Jewish past compel Jews today to identify with that appeal. The lessons of the Jewish past compel them to oppose, with all their being, a demand to annihilate another people.

That belief is clearly articulated in one of Isaac Bashevis Singer's short stories: "A voice from heaven should be ignored if it is not on the side of justice," the renowned Jewish author wrote.[166] The Talmud deals at length with the validity of instructions conveyed by "a heavenly voice"—instructions coming straight from heaven—and for the most part, concludes they shouldn't be listened to. It's man who decides. Man is authorized to decide even if the voice says something different.[167] In other words, if someone believes that man has the authority to suggest a more current interpretation of "Jewish values"—to make those values more in tune with the conscience of the twenty-first-century Jew—he will not be the first and can rely on earlier sources. And many do want to believe that.

For example, Jewish women (also supported by men), who in the last century have fought to achieve emancipation from the chains of Jewish tradition to fashion an active and creative role for themselves in their communities.[168] Some women insisted on studying, assumed rabbinical leadership roles, demanded a different status in the synagogue, could rule on matters of Jewish law, and are changing the reality of family life. These women have no doubt produced a dramatic revolution in daily Jewish life—in all its denominations, ranging from the progressives to the ultra-Orthodox. These women are revising Judaism to make it more palatable to modern-day worldviews and lifestyles.[169]

Thus, we can debate whether or not preferring one's conscience is an act of adherence to Jewish values that rests on theological or philosophical foundations. But you can't argue with the fact that, from a sociological perspective, these conscience-driven decisions are in practice "Jewish values"—in the sense that they determine how a large number of Jews conduct themselves (that is to say, these are Jewish values because they are the values of many Jews).

Here's a short and far from exhaustive list of Jewish values that are rooted in very ancient texts—the Torah and the Books of the Prophets—and which are generally not disputed.[170] Most of them were further enhanced over the course of the Jewish historical experience.

The value of human dignity: the recognition that mankind, all human beings, are created in the image of God.

The value of liberty: Jews were commanded to remember when they were slaves and strangers in foreign lands and were expected to adapt their behavior to the lessons drawn from those memories (but they weren't commanded to abstain from owning slaves, and also had no problem coercing people to fulfill the Commandments).[171]

The value of memory: For many years, the Jews have made sure to be a people that remember. In modern times, the memory of the Holocaust is a key and prominent expression of that value among Jews.[172]

The value of learning: The original Pentateuchal teaching is to study the Torah, but there is, however, a basic value associated with imparting other kinds of knowledge.[173]

Values that establish the right to property: For many generations, Jews had a very difficult time protecting their property from the vagaries of rulers, a hardship that no doubt reinforced their adherence to this value.[174]

The value of family: Forming and raising a family was something Jews always strived to do.

The value of mutual responsibility: at a minimum, mutual responsibility within the Jewish people, which the Talmud finds in the Book of Leviticus, which says, "And they shall fall one upon another." Regarding this, the Talmud says, "It teaches us that all Jews are responsible for one another."[175] The Jews' experience as a minority group during their long years of exile taught them to underscore the power inherent in that value.

All of the above are agreed-upon Jewish values. And they are also values that are now part of the Western global discourse. So what makes them *Jewish* values? Jews have learned over the generations how to communicate with the dominant values of civilization as a whole in three main ways:

The first is the substantive way: by claiming ownership of the values. Granted, Jews and non-Jews share the values in question, but one can locate their source in Jewish tradition. So Jews feel they belong to them. For example, the historian Simon Dubnow wrote that "the exalted idea of One God applied to social life produces the principle of the equality of all men before the One Supreme Power."[176] In other words, the value of equality, which today is a Western value, is originally a Jewish value. The Jewish idea of a covenant can also be viewed as an expression of a "basic ethical idea" that is now embraced worldwide: "…which in itself embodies a basic value: the idea that humans establish institutions and relationships on grounds of a fundamental equality and based upon freely choosing to do so."[177]

The second way to explain the coexistence of Jewish values and the accepted universal values of the period is through interpretation—to propose a Jewish version. The values may be shared, but the rationale underlying them differs for Jews and non-Jews. For instance, in the context of a discussion about welfare policy, some may advocate "reallocating wealth" as a justified reason to impose higher taxes on the rich—an explanation that would be hard to root in Jewish sources. On the other hand, some people may support raising taxes based on the Jewish demand for "basic human compassion" between human beings (which is fundamentally different, even though the two approaches could produce a similar outcome).[178]

The third way to combine the values is by dressing them up as Jewish. The values may be shared and the motivations underlying them identical, but Jews will prefer to dress them in Jewish attire. On occasion, it's done to meet a rhetorical need—to win points in a public debate concerning a disputed issue (e.g., the majority of Jews in the United States support gun control and some of their spiritual leaders maintain that their position stems from Jewish sources).[179] And sometimes it's done even when there's no practical rhetorical benefit, but simply to enrich the cultural discourse.

Some attempts to make Jewish values compatible with the values of the zeitgeist are on display in the ongoing debate about a clash between "Jewish values" and "democratic values" in the way Israel conducts itself. Many Jews fear such a clash, so a simple solution has been found: democracy has been elevated to the stature of a Jewish value by identifying sources that facilitate that interpretation. To illustrate, here is a brief story about the political circus that took place in Israel in the 1980s surrounding the demand to disqualify Rabbi Meir Kahane's party because it espoused illegal racist views.[180]

In the 1980s, the Central Elections Committee received demands to disqualify two parties running for the Knesset: the Progressive List for Peace, a Jewish-Arab party, because it allegedly sought to undermine the existence of Israel as a Jewish state, and Kach, which was founded by Kahane, and allegedly opposed democratic values.[181] Section 7(a) of the Basic Law: The Knesset created an explicit legal foundation for disqualifying parties that deny the existence of Israel as a Jewish state, deny its democratic nature, or incite racism. Accordingly, in 1988, the Supreme Court disqualified Kahane's party list.[182]

"The existence of Israel as the state of the Jewish people does not negate its democratic character," wrote Meir Shamgar, the then-president of the Supreme Court. His fellow justice, Menachem Elon, wrote that Judaism does not allow discrimination against non-Jews or infringement of their right to civil equality or their right to participate in the democratic process. The ruling by the court was a response to Kahane's position—which was exasperating but also interesting. Kahane didn't deny that he was anti-democratic. Rather, he claimed that his anti-democratic views were an authentic articulation of Jewish values. And given those Jewish values, the Jewish state had no grounds for banning his views from being represented in the Knesset.

The State of Israel, through its court system, rejected that argument. Namely, in the legal reality that prevails today in

Israel, the state is unwilling to accept any interpretation that maintains that there is a clash between Jewish values and democratic values, even if it recognizes that such an interpretation exists. And, of course, not only did the court reject that argument, but so do a large majority of Jews across the globe. In their eyes, democracy is a Jewish value, and a betrayal or compromise of democratic values is a betrayal of Judaism itself.[183]

With some help from Jewish tradition, that position can be defended because "Jewish sources contain far more democratic elements, or at least proto-democratic elements, than one might expect."[184] Accordingly, the democracy that prevails in the Jewish state also stems "from deep historical roots."[185] It's an authentic product of Jewish values due to several reasons: the well-known Jewish tradition that says, "the multitude is to be followed;"[186] the sages who comprised the Sanhedrin served in an institution reminiscent of a representative democracy; later on, "in the days of the First Temple and the Second Temple, a model of 'ancient Oriental tyranny' did not emerge in Jewish culture"—and in the days of the ancient Hebrews, Jewish culture was less hierarchal compared to that of other nations; and the "principle underlying the concept of a Jewish regime"—namely, a principle of "public consent."[187]

Think about family values. About the value of helping those less fortunate. Think about the value of the sanctity of life. Think about what American Jews consider an essential part of their Judaism—"working for justice and equality."[188] They are all worthy values that require interpretation. All these values were established in the past and require interpretation in the present. And that interpretation can be found in a variety of places, some even unexpected—in Washington, DC, for instance.

In 2015, when relations between Israel and the United States were somewhat strained, the American president, Barack Obama, came to the Adas Israel synagogue in Washington, DC, to address the congregation in honor of American Jewish Heritage Month.[189] As usual, Obama's speech was splendidly crafted. The word "values" was mentioned in that speech at least twenty times.

The president wanted to convince American Jews that they share an ethical path. He also wanted to intimate that Israel doesn't suitably adhere to Jewish values.[190] Those intimations primarily had a political objective. But it's also possible that the president thought he was describing the situation as it is and that he's an authorized commentator who can decide which Jewish values Israel should be abiding by. President Joe Biden, speaking in 2024, similarly connected "Jewish values" such as "compassion, kindness, and dignity and human life" to his teams' "critical humanitarian assistance" to Palestinians living in Gaza during the war of Israel against Hamas—an issue upon which the US administration and the Israeli government did not share the same view.[191]

The value system that Obama, Biden, and most Jewish Americans share is the set of "Jewish values" that the Presidents believe is rooted in Judeo-Christian tradition.[192] Since the beginning of their American journey, Jews in the United States have been accustomed to believing that there is "nothing incompatible between being a good Jew and a good American." In practice, "for a Jew, the better an American one is, the better Jew one is."[193] Consequently, the Jewish and American sets of values have converged and nearly coalesced according to the historian Jonathan Sarna, who offers some very colorful examples: on Thanksgiving in 1887, a Reform educator described "the Jewish form of government" as being "republican;" in 1891, a rabbi in Cincinnati declared that "Judaism is in perfect harmony with the law of the land;" a Sephardic cantor from the Mikveh Israel synagogue preached "with the spangled banner of liberty in one hand, and the law of Horeb in the other." Jewish values are American values. American values are Jewish values. This is a convenient situation, of course, for all those who are both Jews and Americans, who enjoy a single set of values that suits the diverse identity with which they pave their path in the world.

American Jews distanced themselves from the idea of the "chosen people" once they realized (from sermons and articles in the secular and Christian press and also in other places) that it wasn't beneficial to their image in society.[194] That, too, was a case of value assimilation. Professor Arnold Eisen, who has painstakingly chronicled the subject, starts his book with a delightful story about Joseph Jonas, one of the first American Jews to settle west of the Allegheny Mountains. "One day he encountered an elderly Quaker woman who had never laid eyes on a Jew and was rather excited by the prospect. 'Art thou a Jew? Art thou one of God's chosen people?' she asked. She turned him round and round and at last exclaimed, with evident disappointment, 'Well, thou art no different to other people!'"

The issue of being different is a topic worthy of more thought. Are Jewish values, as interpreted today, actually identical to the values of all Americans or to the values of the Christian tradition? Or is something still distinct about them that is unique to Judaism? In Obama's speech, Jewish values were suspiciously similar to his own set of values. So, on the one hand, his speech was sweet to the ear because it's no trivial matter when the most powerful person in the world praises Jewish values. On the other hand, it was not difficult to notice that the values of the Judaism he was referring to are like those of any other religion he may talk about and are also wondrously reminiscent of everything Obama himself believes in.

Coupled with the values shared by Judaism and civilization as a whole, are there still values on which the Jews have some degree of exclusivity—values that distinguish the Jews from other cultures?

The Jewish ethos underscores the Jews' insistence on creating a culture that is apart from the culture of the rest of the world. In the books of the Bible, there is sharp criticism of the theology and politics of the ancient world.[195] Jews shunned the prevailing fashion and fended off—or at least kept at arm's length—the values that every other culture and religion subscribed to. They said no to paganism and Hellenism, no to the leading religions, including their various sects. In the last two centuries, Jews have taken part, in large numbers, in different movements and campaigns that sought to change the world. However, when looking today for Jewish values that are not embraced by civilization as a whole, or at least not in the Western world, it's not easy to find them. It's not clear that any are left: either the world assimilated values that originated in Judaism (most of them spread from Judaism to Christianity, and from there to European liberalism and humanism), or the Jews incorporated values whose origin wasn't necessarily Jewish (following the change in their status and being accepted as equal citizens in secular nation-states).

Nevertheless, one can still argue, or at least hope, that something of the rebellious spirit has remained with the Jews, which is embodied in two opposing trends. Around half of the Jews—many Israelis and conservative Jews worldwide—are wary and continue to shun some of the ethical trends prevalent in the West (for example, universalist tendencies, whereas conservative Jews prefer to cling to tribalism). The other half—the majority of Jews in the United States and liberal Jews from other communities—are characterized by their highly enthusiastic devotion to certain Western values (compared to any other group, they voice more liberal views about almost every issue under discussion).[196]

In other words, there are Jews whose rebellion against the rest of the world involves saying a more resounding no, and there are Jews whose rebellion means saying a more resounding yes.[197]

By reviewing public opinion surveys and articles and observing how Jewish communities and institutions conduct themselves, one can better understand which values Jews embrace today. Political messages can be extracted from that understanding.[198] And Israeli leaders repeatedly enlist "Jewish values" to promote different and often opposing agendas. One Israeli politician, a known supporter of a free market economy, advocates for "an economy founded on Jewish values."[199] Another Israeli politician, who is a known supporter of the welfare state, also maintains that "Jewish sources can provide the best economic theory."[200] Thus, the question goes back not only to who is the authorized commentator on Jewish values and what their interests are, but also to the essence of the interpretation: are there Jewish values that dictate certain behaviors or policies—for instance, a particular economic policy?

Jewish texts are replete with appeals to help the less fortunate and give charity. Those are Jewish values. The texts also sanction communal coercion to collect charity and give it to the poor.[201] Accordingly, when explaining the "values that underlie its work," the Israeli Ministry of Social Affairs and Social Services claims that its goal is to "safeguard the principles of a welfare state based on the values appearing in the Proclamation of Independence, in the spirit of the vision of the prophets…"[202] But all of the above are statements of a rather general nature and it's hard to find guidelines within them for any specific action, such as how much assistance should be given by the government, who should be the beneficiary of such assistance, under what circumstances should it be extended, etc.

Some Jews believe that the welfare state is the modern manifestation of the vision of the prophets and the fulfillment of key Jewish values of mutual assistance. Some even go so far as to assert that "Jewish and Judeo-socialist ideas should be implemented in a Jewish state," whereas "privatization and competition" are not ideas compatible with a Jewish state because they "reembody Christian-Protestant ideas."[203] Others offer a well-reasoned worldview that is based on a careful examination of Jewish sources, and their conclusion is completely the opposite: "Not only does the welfare state not derive from Jewish sources; rather, as regards some critical points, it is the antithesis of them."[204]

So, as we see, the problems pile up when trying to translate many general Jewish values into a clear language of what to do and what not to do.

One such difficulty arises from the fact that most of the values in question are exceedingly general. "As envisioned by the prophets" is the notion that appears in Israel's Declaration of Independence as a source of inspiration for the foundations of "freedom, justice and peace." But what exactly is the "vision of the prophets" in practical terms—there is no consensus about that (nor were the prophets always of a singular mind). One person will say a welfare state, whereas someone else will say not a welfare state. One will say that "moral sensitivity is more important than strict ritual observance," whereas someone else will disagree and propose that the "Jews be distinct from the peoples surrounding them."[205]

Another difficulty stems from the fact that sets of "Jewish values"—if they exist—were formulated in different periods that are unlike the present one. Therefore, they often do not facilitate drawing a road map that can be used to address modern-day challenges.

A good example of that are the dilemmas pertaining to the use of force by the State of Israel, especially so following the tragedy of the October 7, 2023, attack on Israel and the ensuing war in Gaza, Lebanon, and Iran.[206] The essence of the problem is this: Israel is a country with a Jewish majority, which is founded on "Jewish values" as its population interprets them.[207] But Israel's ability to establish its military doctrine on "Jewish values" is limited. Safeguarding human life appears in Jewish texts. Judaism also prohibits killing. Coupled with that prohibition, there is also the value of protecting the lives of Jews.[208] As is written in Ecclesiastes, "There is a time for war"—in other words, on occasion, one value must be chosen at the expense of another.[209] Sometimes there's a need for "a person to kill and a person to be killed" even though both those acts are tantamount to "violations of the Torah."[210] Furthermore, Jewish history and its lessons don't necessarily provide a key to the appropriate use of force. On the one hand, they are a warning signal to humanity against the improper use of force. On the other hand, they are a warning to Jews that if they don't defend themselves—no one else will.

The professor of Jewish Thought, Aviezer Ravitzky, posited that the prohibition on war "is the starting point for any specific discussion" about battlefield ethics, according to Jewish sources. But what's beyond that general starting point? Maybe not much. As put rather bluntly by the American theorist and philosopher Michael Walzer, "There is no Jewish theory of war and peace." And even if that is an exaggeration, it's clear that a Jewish theory of war and peace relies on very few sources, and only a limited ability exists to derive practical guidelines from them that are relevant to our day and age.[211] None of this is surprising given the circumstances under which Jewish history evolved and Jewish values were fashioned. Throughout most of their history, Jews were unable to go to war, so they didn't have to engage in discussions about military ethics in any actual context.[212]

Nonetheless, many Jews have opinions that are founded on the assumption that they understand what Jewish values are, including their practical implications. A majority of Jews in Israel maintain that Jewish tradition has an impact on their views on subjects such as welfare and helping the needy. Around one-third maintain that Jewish tradition affects their views on protecting the environment.[213] And when it comes to the law of war, Jews also have a general opinion about the role played by Jewish values. They believe, for example, that Jewish values set a high bar for wartime conduct. Even at the height of the post-October 7 war, most Jewish Israelis agreed that the IDF must "meet the objective of a raid while making an effort not to harm the innocent."[214] Only a negligible minority of Jews seem to think that Jewish values embody a demand for a "lower level of ethical conduct" than what international law stipulates.[215]

This is not surprising and is quite similar to what we see in other contexts of the discourse about the significance of Jewish values. More than two-thirds of the Jews living in the United States say that "living an ethical and moral life" is "essential to their sense of Jewishness." And more than half say that "working for justice and equality" is also "essential" to what being Jewish means to them. Put simply, Jews' interpretation of the values they associate with themselves typically includes a demand for ethical excellence. They set an especially high bar of conduct during times of war. They set an especially high bar for leading an ethical life.

This chapter opens with a quote that reflects a sharp difference of opinion.[216] On the one side are the famous words of Rabbi Akiva, who says, "love your neighbor as yourself," and paints it as a "cardinal principle" of the Torah. On the other side are the not-so-famous words of Ben Azzai, who talks about an "even greater principle" that relies on a verse in Genesis: "This is the book of the generations of Adam, on the day that God created man, in the likeness of God He created him."

According to a number of commentators, Rabbi Akiva was referring to the rather small group of Jews when he said "neighbors," whereas Ben Azzai was referring to any man. To every man. Ben Azzai's greater principle is more in sync with the universal tendencies of certain Jews, whereas Rabbi Akiva's cardinal principle is more suitable to the tribal inclinations of other Jews. Another interpretation that informs this debate underlines the passive nature of Ben Azzai's way of thinking.[217] According to his cardinal rule, a man has an inherent "right" ("on the day that God created man")—in the spirit of the modern discourse pertaining to "rights"—as opposed to the active nature of Rabbi Akiva's way of thinking, who says that man has an "obligation" ("love your neighbor") in a more conservative spirit. Either way, both of these sages offer a fundamental ethical principle. It's a principle whose ramifications are vague, like most of the values established by Jewish sages.

These values are general in nature. Judaism doesn't rejoice over going to war; it espouses caring for the less fortunate and helping strangers; it disapproves of tyranny and slavery, and it believes in dialogue and debate.

But do these values facilitate the formulation of a clear stance on the right course of action? That's less certain. As Hillel the Elder said when he established another cardinal principle in the Torah, "what is hateful to you, do not do to others," and "now go and learn."[218]

JEWISH VALUES: A ROAD MAP

They exist or don't exist

Values don't exist: there is the Torah and what is written in it (and the set of commandments deriving from it)—those are Jewish values.

Values exist: they appear in Jewish traditions or in the lessons drawn from the Jewish past; one needs to find them and act according to them.

Jews exist: Jewish values are the values that Jews believe in

(today, primarily Western values).

What's Jewish about our values

We were here first: Judaism invented the universal values that are commonly accepted today.

We have our own interpretation: the values may be similar, but our explanations of them are different.

We have our own sources: every value can be wrapped in a suitable Jewish cover.

Question 4:

Why Do They Hate Us?

Rabbi Shimon ben Yochai said: It is a well-known law that Esau hates Jacob.
(Rashi on Genesis 33:4)[219]

On March 25, 1144, in England, the forester Henry de Sprowston took a ride on his horse looking for people "who may be making mischief or, more likely, cutting timber without a license."[220] He was looking for scoundrels but found a body in the woods—the body of a 12-year-old boy.

The English boy was later known as William of Norwich. Who killed him and discarded his body? We'll never know. But we do know that Jews were blamed for the murder. Five years after the local incident, a monk named Thomas of Monmouth wrote his account of the events and made it known beyond Norwich.[221] He claimed that young William was the victim of a ritual in which some local Jews—at the time, around 200 of them lived in the busy city—reenacted the Crucifixion of Christ, using the child.

That is the earliest record of a *blood libel* against Jews, a tall tale that has repeated itself thousands of times since then. In many such instances, young boys were involved— whether the death of 12-year-old William of Norwich or the death of 13-year-old Andrei Yushchinsky from Kyiv.[222] Yushchinsky was the victim of a murder that led to the most notorious blood libel of the twentieth century, launched against the Jew Mendel Beilis in Russia in 1913.[223]

The plots in most of the blood libels are identical. The only element that changes is the name of the victim. In some of them, the Jew is not prosecuted. That's what happened in Norwich in the twelfth century. In others, the Jew is acquitted. That's what happened in Czarist Russia in the twentieth century. And in some cases, there isn't even a body. That's what happened in the town of La Guardia in Spain in 1491, in an incident that ultimately resulted in the accused Jews being burned at the stake.[224] Regardless of the circumstances, the traces of ancient blood libels still linger. Some aspect of them continues to haunt the Jews. It's present in folklore, art, and the perception of the Jewish people that has become pervasive across the globe.

There is a multitude of groundless allegations concerning Jewish customs, from Norwich to Kyiv to lands as distant as Syria, the site of the Damascus Affair.[225] The willingness of citizens to believe in what *The New York Times* editorial about the Beilis trial described as a "foolish and blind superstition" must astonish the sensible observer.[226] And yet, it's clear that such foolishness had the power to endanger Jewish lives for centuries. And the outcome of the sham trials didn't always make a difference: the resounding acquittal of Beilis was later used by the

Nazis as evidence of the Jews' guile and cunning because they managed to prevail even over powerful Russia.[227] The Damascus Affair provided antisemitic groups with "conclusive evidence that ritual murder and human sacrifice played an essential role in the practices of a small sect of Jews, if not a greater number."[228]

Numerous volumes have been devoted to the question of antisemitism, a phenomenon that arouses amazement, if not disbelief. Why has the hatred of Jews lasted so long?

There is no definitive answer. This hatred—"an outrage to common sense" as the German-born Jewish philosopher Hannah Arendt put it—has roots and reasons. One can seek explanations for it. But it's worth acknowledging from the start: one can explain antisemitism at a particular moment in time; it's more difficult to explain it at all moments in time.

Some explanations focus on the practical, calculated and utilitarian angles.

Blood libels, which are just one component of an appalling and familiar collection of antisemitic incidents, often emerged against the backdrop of local, political, and religious circumstances. The story of William of Norwich spread quickly during a civil war in England and following the failed Second Crusade.[229] The La Guardia blood libel also blended in well with the *realpolitik* that characterized the reign of Ferdinand and Isabella just four months before the edict expelling the Jews from Spain was issued.[230] One can occasionally identify an objective, real or imagined, that those circulating the hatred wished to achieve. Sometimes, it could be an estate owner who wanted to eliminate the debt he owed to local Jews. Or it could be a political leader who needed a scapegoat to blame for his failures. However, sometimes there was no gain, or the loss even exceeded the gain. That's what the Turkish sultan found surprising after he heard about the expulsion of the Jews from Spain: "How can you call Ferdinand of Aragon a wise king—the same Ferdinand who impoverished his land and enriched ours?"[231] Turkey had absorbed some Spanish Jews, and the sultan was glad to gain what the Spaniards lost.

Some explanations focus on matters relating to faith and lifestyle.

In ancient times, the Jews refused to adapt to the pagan world, and, in later generations, they refused to assimilate into their Christian or Muslim surroundings. Not only did that set them apart, but it also rendered them outsiders who were a constant, persistent, and often annoying reminder that not everyone accepted the prevailing religion of the time and its universal aspirations.[232] Jews didn't completely integrate, and they were conspicuously different in a number of ways. They didn't eat the same food (due to dietary laws) and rested when everyone else was working (on the Sabbath). There were times when Jews actively resisted attempts to force them to assimilate (in the days of the Hasmoneans), or on occasion they preferred to die as "martyrs" rather than assimilate (during the Crusades and also in Yemen).[233] These cases are famous because they are extreme: Those knowledgeable in Jewish law understood that suicide is a transgression and not only turned a blind eye when Jews took their own lives but also when they took their wives' and children's lives as well, to avoid conversion.[234]

Starting in ancient times and up to the beginning of the modern period, Jews mostly lived in communities that were set apart. And that didn't always make their neighbors any fonder of them. In the winter of 38 AD or 39 AD, a delegation led by a scholar named Apion from Alexandria, Egypt, traveled to Rome for an audience with the emperor Caligula, where he argued against the Jews.[235] At the time, the residents of Alexandria were divided into two classes: the privileged citizens from the Greek ruling class and the locals who lacked citizenship. The Jewish citizens "were an exception, an anomaly."[236] They had separate institutions and their way of life was different. "If they are citizens, why don't the Jews worship the same gods as the rest of the Alexandrians?" asked Apion. Philo of Alexandria—a highly respected Jew dispatched to Rome to refute Apion's accusations—was granted only a brief audience with the emperor. In all probability, Caligula would have ruled against the Jews if he hadn't been assassinated first. The decision made by his successor, Claudius, was much less harsh from the Jews' perspective: they would not be considered citizens but would not lose their political rights.

Some explanations of Jew-hatred focus on its psychological roots. Due to the Nazi persecution of the Jews, Sigmund Freud was forced to leave his home in Vienna and move to London, where he died a year later. In his book *Moses and Monotheism*, Freud offers an interpretation of Jew-hatred, claiming that Christians have an oedipal relationship with Jews. Judaism is the father religion, and Christianity is the rebellious son.[237] Later explanations that are not decidedly Freudian also view the psyche and human consciousness as keys to understanding antisemitism. Many of them highlight how the existence of Judaism played into the hands of those who had a hard time deciphering a puzzling and erratic world in times of crisis. Antisemitism becomes deadly "only when a culture, nation or faith suffers from a cognitive dissonance so profound that it becomes unbearable," wrote Rabbi The Lord Jonathan Sacks.[238] With the Christians, it intensified as Islam grew in strength. In Germany, it happened after its defeat in World War I. These were events that required an explanation. Blaming the Jews is a certain kind of explanation.

Hence, the Jews played the role of the villain in the eyes of the communists, who viewed them as a gang of bourgeoisie capitalists — The Jews were the moneylenders who got rich at the country's expense—but they were also the wretched who impeded economic growth.[239] "Destitute and dressed in rags…" is how the Jews fleeing to Germany from the pogroms in 1881 were depicted.[240] They were too strong or too weak, too tribal or too dispersed. Some Western thinkers considered them the enemies of morality and the enemies of progress, whereas others, such as Adolf Hitler, believed the Jews cunningly managed to subjugate the world to their morality, which of course is Jewish and therefore undesirable.[241]

There is the type of antisemitism that leaves an opening, a way out for Jews: by converting, assimilating, integrating, and losing parts of their identity. Shylock, in Shakespeare's *The Merchant of Venice*, is a character who has a way out. At least some people who read the play view him as a greedy, petty, and deceitful moneylender. But, "Shylock can be saved."[242] All he has to do is convert from being a bad Jewish man to a Christian who changes his ways.

But there's also a hatred of Jews which doesn't leave them a way out—a hatred they cannot avoid due to their inborn, inherited traits. Charles Dickens's Fagin in *Oliver Twist*, another despicable fictional Jew of classic literature, is such a character.[243] He lures children into becoming thieves, has a foul odor, and, in Dickens's words, a "repulsive" face. Fagin is representative of Jewish wickedness compared to innocent Englishness.[244] But there's a difference between Fagin and Shylock. Fagin is a scoundrel "by nature" who can't be rehabilitated.

The explanations for antisemitism shift over time, but antisemitism itself doesn't seem to have an expiration date. It assumes one form and then sheds it; it intensifies in a new locale while growing weaker in another. Many of the derogatory images attributed to Jews have remained in place: there's a straight line that connects works of art in Christian medieval Europe with caricatures found in the Muslim world today. There's also a line that connects the first-century Roman philosopher Seneca, who called the Jews a "criminal tribe," with the nineteenth-century, Jew-hating German composer Richard Wagner, who believed there was a "harmful influence of Jewry on the morality of the nation."[245]

Jew-haters have, of course, always maintained that the source of their hostility is Jewish behavior. Quite a few Jews have agreed with that assertion, sometimes as a result of a supposedly dispassionate analysis of so-called facts, but mostly because they've internalized how Jews are perceived by non-Jews. So, what we have here is a highly sensitive topic for discussion in any Jewish forum: to what extent are the Jews themselves responsible—due to their customs, their behavior—for the hatred directed against them? Have the Jews been "absolutely beyond reproach, or do they bear a bit of the blame for the calamities that have befallen them?"[246]

The French Jewish philosopher and essayist Bernard Lazare, who was one of the first to publicly maintain that Captain Alfred Dreyfus (of the 1894 Dreyfus Affair) was innocent of treason, wrote that Jews were wrong to "rebel only against persecution from without and not against oppression from within." In other words, as he saw it, the ones making the Jews miserable were Jewish leaders who had vested interests in keeping the Jews in their pitiful state." In his book *Antisemitism: Its History and Causes*, Lazare wrote that "the Jews were themselves, in part, at least, the cause of their own ills."[247] Many Zionist leaders agreed with him. Antisemitism has causes, and as the visionary of the Jewish state, Theodor Herzl, put it, "the first cause is that, throughout the many generations of persecutions, we lost our ability to totally assimilate."[248] Jews suffer because they didn't take the necessary steps to end the suffering. They suffer because they insist on dwelling among other nations who will naturally develop animosity toward outsiders.[249]

Nevertheless, the same question comes up again: Why this animosity? Those who wanted to pin the blame on the victims of hatred found reasons to do so: the Jews' arrogance, their insistence on leading a different lifestyle, and the revolutionary ideas they brought with them, which at times conflicted with those of the local population. But as the American essayist Leon Wieseltier put it, the problem is not in the "Jewish insistence upon difference, but in the non-Jewish insistence on sameness."[250] If Jewish difference provokes antisemitism, as early as in the days of Haman from the Book of Esther ("their laws are different from those of every other people"[251]), it was never about the failure of Jews to be like other people, but the challenge of tolerance they posed to them.

One thing is clear: A "stimulus-response relationship" existed between the Jews and the non-Jews they lived among.[252] The noticeable presence of Jews—especially when they were financially or socially successful, or when they filled a key role in dramatic changes (capitalism, communism), or when the surrounding society faced a crisis for which reasons had to be found—is the stimulus. Antisemitism, in varying degrees of severity, is the response. According to the historian Bernard Lewis, there was a "recurring tendency in Islamic sources to attribute subversive and extremist doctrines to Jewish origins." For example, they were presented by certain haters as having a hand in the schism within Islam (a bitter and deadly divide between the two main streams of Islam, Sunni and Shi'a, originated with a dispute over who should succeed the Prophet Muhammad as leader of the faith).[253]

Jews, more than anyone else, have suffered the pitfalls of this hatred. They have and continue to pay for it in blood or in heavy financial tolls, in the assimilation of those who were weary of withstanding hostile forces, in unavoidable self-flagellation, and in an emotional burden that conveys anxiety about the future, as well as in the cultural shift of Judaism to focusing on disasters. The Jews' formative experience in the last century was the Holocaust. And still today, for many, remembering the Holocaust is the most "essential part of what being Jewish means to them."[254] Perhaps they're exaggerating. Some historians—Salo Baron was the trailblazer in this area—believe that the Jews misread their history and have a "lachrymose" conception of it. Jewish history has had its share of colossal tragedies—but according to Baron, the majority of Jewish history has not been tragic.[255]

But even Baron can't deny that antisemitism exists. Antisemitism forced the Jewish people to contend with the onslaught of violence and discrimination, and that reckoning yielded two survival mechanisms.[256]

The first—the fine-tuning of the elements of Jewish identity against the backdrop of a hostile world. "The rank and file of a people are instructed by revolutions and catastrophes better than by sermons," wrote the historian Simon Dubnow, who identified these shifts even in the Babylonian Exile: "More quickly than Isaiah and Jeremiah, Nebuchadnezzar brought the Jews to a recognition of their tasks."[257] The second—the practical prevention of assimilation and the preservation of ways of life. "The ghetto offered security and even comfort of a kind," wrote the historian Paul Johnson when describing the condition of the Jews in the Middle Ages. The ghetto was an expression of the non-Jews' desire to segregate the Jews. But, at the same time, it also "made the observance of the law (the *mitzvoth*) easier in many ways." Johnson and numerous others view the segregation of the Jews—whose original purpose was to "safeguard Christians from evil Jewish contacts"—as something that "protected Jews from secularity."[258] The hatred of a particular group underscores the existence of that group. Thus, antisemitism—which in many of its phases reflected a wish to be rid of the Jews and encouraged many of them to distance themselves from Judaism—undoubtedly also filled some sort of role in achieving the opposite objective: it preserved the Jews as a group that does not assimilate.[259]

The persecution of the Jews drove them to settle in places where the vast majority of them still live: North America and Israel. Although Jews emigrated from Europe to the new continent primarily for economic reasons, those financial hardships were born of the antisemitic discrimination they faced.[260] In the case of Israel, the persecution of the Jews played a direct role. Between the Jewish Enlightenment and the Jewish Emancipation, Jews dreamed of progress that would eradicate antisemitism, but such hopes turned into disappointment. Jews continued to look for a solution, and some believed that the only long-term option was a separate national entity—which would provoke a fundamental change in the Jewish "condition." That's how the movement of immigrants from Europe to Palestine was born. That's how 90 percent of the Jews in Iraq chose to leave their country and move to Israel within two years.[261]

But when it comes to uprooting antisemitism, the existence of Israel only complicated matters further. Today, Israel is the main explanation and excuse for displays of antisemitism around the world. Israel's very presence in the Middle East inflames the Muslim world, and also groups in Western countries against

Israeli Jews in particular and Jews in general. This was evident in the 2024 eruption of aggressive anti-Israel campus protests across the United States.[262] In addition, Israel's very existence, regardless of its location, fuels suspicions about the Jews' supposed dual loyalty: to their own countries and Israel.

Because charges of questionable loyalty led to the persecution of Jews in the past, such accusations still shock and terrify every Jewish community around the world. In 1919, when a delegation of Jews headed by Chaim Weizmann was invited to present their demands at the Paris Peace Conference, they were amazed to hear the testimony of Sylvain Levi, the representative from the Jewish-French organization Kol Israel Haverim (Alliance). He spoke against the idea of a national home, claiming that the Land of Israel is too small to take in millions of Jews and that the establishment of a Jewish political center would "introduce the dangerous principle of Jewish dual loyalties."[263] American Jewish organizations shared a similar concern in the pre-State period.[264] In 1950, Jacob Blaustein, the president of the American Jewish Committee, demanded a commitment from Israeli Prime Minister David Ben-Gurion that "nothing be said or done by Israel that would create, or give the impression of creating, any dual loyalty on the part of American Jews."[265] Following the establishment of the State of Israel, Arab countries were emptied of their prosperous Jewish communities that had lived there for hundreds of years. Among other things, it reflected a "genuine fear" within Arab states of "the subversive capacity of the Jews, who were suspected of identifying with Zionism and with Israel."[266] Subsequent events, such as the role played by Jewish officials in the US administration in planning the war in Iraq,[267] or the Israeli government's encouragement of French Jews[268] to move to Israel, intensified Jewish concerns about being accused of dual loyalty.

Antisemitism has once again changed its state and adapted its messages to the Israeli era.[269] If the Jews of the Middle Ages were a disquieting element because they didn't have a place of their own, then the Jews of the modern age are a disquieting element because they insist on having a place of their own. Not only has antisemitism not expired following the establishment of the State of Israel, on the contrary, its generators have found in the State of Israel a rather convenient propaganda tool to spread their messages. (And truth must be told: In some cases, Israeli leaders, by words and deed, provided these messengers useful fodder with which to feed the antisemitic beast.)

Israel does, however, offer Jews some sort of refuge when under attack, primarily by giving them the ability to defend themselves. They are no longer dependent on the vagaries of a particular ruler or sudden fluctuations in the mood of non-Jewish majority groups. On the other hand, the hostility continues to require Jews living in Israel to be on the alert, which they've become accustomed to. The massacre of October 7, 2023, was a stark reminder of the consequences of neglecting to be constantly on guard.

And it's worth mentioning that now, too, antisemitism can be explained and characterized based on the particular circumstances of place and time. The philosopher Isaiah Berlin claimed that groups develop strong hatred toward other groups when subjected to persistent historical insult and humiliation by foreign forces stronger than their own.[270] The Arab world at the beginning of the twenty-first century is likely to fit that description. Thus, maybe some of the reasons that the Middle East is the supplier of lethal Jew-hatred today are similar to the reasons that led Europe to supply deadly Jew-hatred at the beginning of the twentieth century.

The bottom line is this: Today, just a few decades after the Holocaust, it appears that even the extreme nature of the Nazis' savagery didn't stamp out antisemitism in the rest of the world. In a rather backwards proposition, Berlin wrote that "for fifty years, Nazism was the protector of the Jews in the West" because Hitler "dishonored anti-Semitism" and delegitimized the hatred of Jews. But it soon became clear that it was only "a temporary pause. Some thought it was a *fait accompli*, but in retrospect it turns out it was just an intermission."[271] Today's antisemitism makes use of delegitimized Nazism to bash Jews: Israeli leaders with long noses in newspaper cartoons are the ones now depicted as being bloodthirsty, devious, and evil. At the beginning of the 1980s, a Soviet caricature portrayed an Israeli prime minister—who had lost most of his family in the Holocaust—as carrying a sign that said *Blitzkreig*, with Hitler standing behind him and smiling.[272]

The large-scale abandonment of Europe and the emigration to North America also did not result in the end of antisemitism. It did, however, put nearly half of the Jewish people in a place where antisemitism seemed to be less of a threat for many decades.[273] With regard to the United States, the big question—which was alluded to above—has two parts: Will the Jews continue to maintain a separate identity even when their surroundings are not antisemitic, and for how long of a period can antisemitism stay dormant? Events occurring in the second and third decades of the twenty-first century might suggest that "the golden age of American Jews is ending," as Franklin Foer proposed.[274]

It's not hatred that made the Jews a people, but its presence helped them preserve a collective identity and a sense of shared destiny. If the hatred goes away, they will have to regroup and find partnerships as well as identity-generating tools tailored to the spirit of the time. Not long ago, some Jewish leaders in America assumed that the time to do such a thing was "now." That was when America was still more clearly a place where Jew-hatred didn't play a major role in the public arena or in shaping the lives of young Jews, and was also a place that surrounded its Jews with acceptance more than any other they have settled in throughout their history. In other words, a safe America (and in 2025, when this edition of the book is prepared, it is still relatively safe, but not as safe as it used to be,) is a place that poses a great challenge to the Jews in their struggle to safeguard "continuity." "I find that I am suddenly living in a country in which the Jew has come to be—or is allowed for now to think he is—a cultural hero," wrote the American-Jewish author Philip Roth.[275] That country and that period in time, and that situation of a close embrace with their non-Jewish surroundings, are also the conditions that test the ability of the Jews to exist as a distinct group over time.[276]

And as for the non-Jews: For two thousand years or more, they became accustomed to using "Jewishness" as the "the most powerful language of opprobrium available to any critic of the powers and institutions of this world."[277] The Jews were a popular punching bag when needed, and Judaism a popular scapegoat when the occasion arose. Such usages became a chronic habit, and the views behind them are deeply ingrained in the non-Jewish consciousness.

Because Jew-hatred has been around for such a long time, it's hard to imagine the world—that of Jews and non-Jews—without it. It's not at all certain that both parties would know how to manage in its absence. The Anti-Defamation League, which documents antisemitic activity, estimated that over 1 billion people in the world today "harbor anti-Semitic attitudes."[278] Many of them believe that "Jews have too much power in the business world," or that "Jews think they are better than other people."[279] A survey conducted by the Pew Research Center found that over 90 percent of people living in Muslim countries have unfavorable views of Jews.[280] In Egypt, 2 percent of the population has a good opinion of Jews. In Jordan—2 percent. In Pakistan—2 percent. In Lebanon—3 percent. According to many studies, antisemitism is also on the rise in Europe.[281] And in the United States. And Australia. And Canada.[282] Antisemitism is the "most enduring of all hatreds," wrote Robert Wistrich in his monumental work, *A Lethal Obsession*.[283]

Ironically, antisemitism is the mirror image of Judaism. It's the mirror image of a civilization with an incredible capacity to adapt to changing circumstances.

REASONS FOR JEW-HATRED AND ITS OUTCOMES

Beliefs: Jews rebel against prevailing trends (Hellenism, Christianity, Islam).

Lifestyle: They set themselves apart, they have different customs, they refuse to assimilate.

Geography: They're dispersed among everyone (or insist on fighting over land that's already taken).

Psychology: They serve as a convenient explanation for those who find it hard to understand a complex world.

Habit: After so many years, why replace the punching bag?

The damage inflicted on Jews is considerable: persecutions and murder, financial hardship, emotional stress, cultural inclination.

But it preserves identity: a sense of a shared destiny, "otherness" that prevents assimilation.

Question 5:

How Do We Survive?

"In every generation they rise up against us to destroy us, and the Holy One, blessed be He, rescues us from their hands."
(Passover Haggadah)

Four months before the end of the nineteenth century, in September 1899, Mark Twain published an intriguing article entitled *Concerning the Jews.*[284]

Twain—who wrote *Tom Sawyer* and *Adventures of Huckleberry Finn*—was in Europe in 1899, closely following the attempts to rescue the Austro-Hungarian Empire from collapse. In the margins of an article in which he described the political earthquake shaking the European continent, Twain also mentioned the ongoing harassment of the Jews, who served as a lightning rod for the anger of the masses.[285] The letters he received following the publication of that article led Twain to write another, separate article just about the Jews. It was dozens of pages long and dealt primarily with the persistent hatred of the Jews.[286] But one can also see the author's wonder at the Jews' resilience despite the frequent challenges that threatened them.

Twain observed that Jews persevered more than other peoples who were purportedly larger and stronger than they were. He wrote: "The Egyptian, the Babylonian, and the Persian rose, filled the planet with sound and splendor, then faded to dream-stuff and passed away; the Greek and the Roman followed and made a vast noise, and they are gone; other peoples have sprung up and held their torch high for a time, but it burned out, and they sit in twilight now, or have vanished. The Jew saw them all, beat them all, and is now what he always was, exhibiting no decadence, no infirmities of age, no weakening of his parts, no slowing of his energies, no dulling of his alert and aggressive mind. All things are mortal but the Jew; all other forces pass, but he remains. What is the secret of his immortality?"

That's a good question. Perhaps one of the most intriguing conundrums in history. Some of Twain's answers can be gleaned from his article: the Jews' family values, mutual assistance, and business integrity. Yes—business integrity. Twain refused to submit to the prevailing image of Jews as shrewd crooks. He thought they were shrewd but also believed their business success was proof of their honesty. His acquaintance with a few famous Jews, including the visionary of the Jewish state, Theodor Herzl (a great admirer of Mark Twain and his stories[287]), no doubt contributed to forming that favorable impression.

Twain was not the first, nor the last, to marvel at the resilience of the Jews in the face of the forces that threatened to eliminate them from the global arena. Whoever gives some thought to that resilience should be puzzled. An abundance of theories proposes factors that can explain why civilizations survive and nations prosper, and the Jews are often one of their case studies.[288] And rightfully so—they are a small and peculiar group that has managed to escape the ravages of time. They are a group who have left history stupefied.

The twentieth-century American historian Max Dimont, who wrote the bestselling book *Jews, God and History,*[289] cited six such existential period-related challenges that the Jews managed to overcome:

The pagan world was the first challenge, where "[the Jews] came perilously close to disappearing."[290] After that, the Jews managed to overcome the temptations of their Greco-Roman surroundings, and "it was a miracle that that the Jews emerged from it all" when the rest of the world was undergoing an accelerated process of Hellenization. The third challenge was the existence of small and separate communities in the Diaspora, joined by "the creation of a religious-legal code." The fourth challenge was Islam, which stormed the world's center stage in the seventh century. Jews often flourished under Muslim rule. The fifth challenge was the 1,200-year period of the Middle Ages and Jewish life under Christian rule. "All non-Christian nations which were defeated in the name of the Cross were converted to the Cross—except the Jews," Dimont wrote. The sixth and last challenge "is the Modern Age itself." Whether or not the Jews will be able to prevail once again is something that remains to be seen. Dimont addressed that question in another book he wrote, *The Indestructible Jews.*[291]

Are they indestructible? Dimont's answer is not clear. In his book, he divides Jewish history into three periods. The two thousand years between Abraham the Patriarch and Jesus, another two thousand years between "Jesus and Ben-Gurion" and then, the next two thousand years—the future.[292]

Regarding each period, Dimont tries to uncover the secret of the Jews' strengths and their contribution to human civilization and its development. Faithful to his discipline, Dimont aimed to provide "an explanation for Jewish survival that is consistent with natural law"—namely, an explanation that not only Jews who believe in a "guiding divinity" can accept.[293] Put simply: Dimont aims to address just one of three possible frameworks that can explain the Jews' resilience.

The first framework is not actually one of explanation: it's a framework that denies the need for an explanation. It's an assumption that can't be substantiated or refuted which says that the Jews' survival is nothing more than a fortunate coincidence.[294] For a number of millennia of human existence, one nation, small in size, managed to survive longer than the others. It may be a matter of chance, and the explanations associated with it are no more than an attempt to explain, after the fact, something that needs no explanation at all.[295]

But even those who believe that Jewish resilience is more than a statistical fluke have a fundamental disagreement, as evidenced by the other two frameworks. On the one side, some subscribe to the supernatural explanation—a divine plan. On the other, some researchers prefer explanations devoid of the divine, such as social circumstances or the impact of beliefs and attitudes, geography, leadership, and economic development—either combined or each one separately.

Professor Yirmiyahu Yovel maintained that "all being a rare and unique historical phenomenon, it is still possible to understand Jewish survival through intelligence and experience without involving divine intervention."[296] And he is, of course, right: numerous researchers have already proven that it is indeed "possible" to try and do that. The question is whether understanding "through intelligence and experience" is not only possible but also the most plausible approach. Or is there a better way to explain the Jewish people's resilience?[297]

A well-known story provides an account of a conversation between the Prussian king Frederick the Great and one of his advisors. The king demanded a single, undisputed proof of the existence of God, to which his advisor replied: "Why, the Jews, your Majesty—the Jews! They are the proof."[298]

That anecdote is an explanation based on a longstanding tradition that attributes the Jews' survival to divine will. It may be a religious explanation—but in this case, it's not a Jewish one.

The teachings of Saint Augustine in early Christian theology maintained that the Roman Catholic Church had to protect the Jews because they are the "witnesses" who can prove the superior power of the new faith to the world.[299] It is God's will that the Jews continue to exist in their defeated wretchedness, like Cain in his day, as a constant reminder of the victory of Christianity.

In modern Christian theology, which is more sympathetic to the Jews, especially among some present-day evangelicals, there is a rejection of "replacement theology," which posits that ever since the Jews rejected Jesus's gospel, God rejected the Jews.

They believe that God's love for the Jews is ongoing, that God didn't abandon them, and that it is His will that they continue to be protected.[300]

And there are, of course, Jewish explanations of the religious variety.

The Jewish explanation can rest on God's will to achieve His objectives through His people. Rabbi Abraham Isaac Hacohen Kook, whose revolutionary approach to the Zionist enterprise still has an enormous impact on Israeli society today, viewed all of Jewish history as an unending process of redemption, guided from above: "a reflection of an inner divine occurrence, where the historical reality is nothing but its outward expression."[301] Rabbi Kook's approach draws from philosophical tenets found in the teachings of Friedrich Hegel and echoes the familiar idea of the "cunning of reason."[302] Throughout history, that cunning has misled human beings who cannot grasp its nature, yet it is directed toward an end God wishes to attain.[303]

The Jewish explanation can also rely on God's commitment to the existence of His people regardless of achieving any particular objective — a commitment that even God himself must keep.[304] According to Rabbi Eleazar, as recounted in Tractate Berakhot in the Babylonian Talmud, that's exactly what Moses asserted when God wanted to destroy the Jewish people following the sin of the Golden Calf.[305] "Moses said to the Holy One, blessed be He: 'Master of the Universe, if You had taken an oath for them [Israel] by heaven and earth, I would have said that just as heaven and earth will be destroyed, so will Your oath be destroyed. But now that You took an oath for them by Your great name, just as Your great name lives and endures forever and ever, so does Your oath endure forever and ever.'" Simply put: If You are eternal, so is Your promise; therefore, your obligation to keep it is also eternal.

So what we see here is divine providence over the Jews that is uplifting and not humiliating, like Saint Augustine's version. Rabbi Eliezer Berkovits regarded this providence as testimony of God's ongoing relationship with human beings.[306] The age of the prophecy has surely passed. Nowadays, we live in a *hester panim* reality, which in Hebrew refers to a time when God does not explicitly reveal himself. But the Jews' extraordinary story—one of a people who spent most of history with no power, with no sovereignty—is what testifies to the existence of divine compassion that exists in our world.[307]

But what if neither chance nor providence brought the Jews this far?

Based on the historians and political philosophers who wrote about the rise and fall of civilizations—ranging from Edward Gibbon in the eighteenth century to Francis Fukuyama in the twenty-first—it seems that no single factor ever built or destroyed an ancient civilization but always a variety of factors.[308] Internal circumstances were often no less important than the pressures exerted on the group from the outside.[309] Jewish history is replete with stories and anecdotes that testify to a combination of such circumstances, endogenous and exogenous, and to qualities of Jewish life that rescued Jews from assimilation and extinction even when faced with tough challenges.

For long periods the presence of Jews was a tolerable, if not good, bargain both for the Jews and for the non-Jewish communities they lived in. In the pagan ancient world, Jews were not perceived as a major threat. In the Muslim world, while not seen nor treated as equal, they were considered a group that made a positive contribution to economic and political stability. In the Christian world, which was more hostile, the Jews were members of one of many classes whose status wasn't particularly high but also wasn't the lowest rung on the ladder. They belonged to a class the rulers had reason to protect because of their contribution to local commerce and the economy.

Nonetheless, pressure and obstacles often escalated. We'll use a story from the fourteenth century to illustrate how the Jews overcame them as well.

During the Spanish Inquisition, a set of laws that sought to persecute or forcibly convert all those deemed heretics by the Catholic Church was implemented. The Jews in Spain didn't convert all at once. Nor did they initially believe that they had no other choice. But the Christians completed their conquest of most of the Iberian Peninsula in the fourteenth century and gradually stepped up their efforts to convert the Jews. The Christians' protective attitude toward the Jews was pushed aside as they became intoxicated with power and elated following their victories. Because the Jews' inferiority had been proven, and because there was also evidence that they were enemies of the religion that was destined to rule the world, if they wanted to live, they had to embrace Christianity.[310]

There were Jews who did just that—some due to a genuine preference for the Christian religion and others due to the weariness following their struggle or simple utilitarian considerations. This was the result of a long but growing process of accepting their fate. However, the wholesale conversion to Christianity only began after nearly a century of attempts by the Catholic authorities.

One could view that as evidence that Jews, like all other human beings, only understand the language of force. The wave of pogroms that broke out in 1391 opened the gates to the torrent of *conversos*—converted Jews—that began flooding Spain. From a small community on the margins of Jewish society, they became a widespread phenomenon. Some believe that roughly 50 percent of all Spanish Jews at the time converted to Christianity. In the city of Valencia, there were rumors that the number of Jews who wanted to convert was so large it would take a miracle to finish converting all of them.[311]

But that strong pressure did not defeat the Jewish people. Neither did the expulsion from Spain which occurred about a hundred years after the pogroms. Why? That question has more than one answer.

The Jews' dispersion precluded any possibility that the Church's victory in Spain would make all Jews vanish, just like such dispersion precluded that possibility in other episodes that occurred in the course of history. Their dispersion rescued many Jews when the Roman Emperor Hadrian imposed decrees on them in the Land of Israel and crushed the Bar Kokhba revolt. During that period of crisis, the Jews in Babylonia were safe under Parthian rule.[312] Their dispersion saved many Jews from annihilation when Nazi Germany sought to wipe out the Jewish people, once and for all—because there were Jews who didn't live in occupied Europe.[313]

Their ideological dispersion—namely, the absence of a uniform way of thinking—also played a role in the story of Jewish survival. It gave the Jews an arena conducive to developing different paths of Judaism. Of course, it remains to be seen which path will lead the Jews forward, and which path will lead to a dead end. However, because Jews never followed the same path, they were never collectively compelled to face any situation from which there was no way out.

Another factor in their survival was the intensity of their faith. Jews trusted their covenant with God which assured their existence, and that thought alone became a propelling force and a self-fulfilling belief.[314] Furthermore, that faith instilled a rebellious obstinacy in at least some Jews when faced with attempts to force them to convert. That was the case in Spain and during other periods as well. During the Hasmonean revolt, for example, that defiance played a decisive role in impeding the Hellenization process in the Land of Israel. Describing the brutal decrees imposed by the Greeks, the nineteenth-century historian Heinrich Graetz wrote that the "cruelties, instead of intimidating the people, only increased their determined resistance" until the Jews initiated an armed rebellion.[315]

Flexibility and pragmatism characterized many of the Jews in Spain, who continued to practice some of their previous customs clandestinely in response to the persistent harassment. The same flexibility and pragmatism were the foundation of the varied reactions to external developments in all periods of Jewish history.[316]

That ritualistic flexibility was devised by Rabbi Yohanan Ben Zakkai, who invented a Judaism that can live without sovereignty and without a Temple.[317, 318] The same flexibility was crucial to the foundation of the Zionist revolution that reinvented the Jews' national existence in a world where the cultural role of religion was being eroded and losing its power. "In the early days of Zionism, the Jewish nationality was a vision and not a fact, a plan and not something real," wrote the historian and author Gadi Taub in his short book, *What is Zionism.*[319] "Zionism was a revolution that defined Jewish identity on a secular basis: nationalism." Flexibility and pragmatism can be seen throughout Jewish history: in the *prosbul* regulation instituted by Hillel the Elder, which circumvented the moratorium on debts every seven years because it was interfering with the normal course of commerce;[320] in the decision to convert the Oral Law into written law, and later even into printed law, to preserve the Jewish people's important spiritual assets;[321] and also in subsequent developments such as the emergence of Orthodox Judaism and Reform Judaism that were a response to the Jewish Enlightenment and the Jewish Emancipation.

The Jews' segregation, both self-imposed and otherwise, as well as the autonomy they were given to adjudicate their own matters, made it easier for them to survive as a distinct, unassimilated group.[322] The hatred of Jews also played a role in history's plan: nearly every contemporary analysis of the Jewish people's ability to survive assigns a place of honor to their biggest haters. Economic discrimination in various periods forced the Jews to specialize in occupations that ultimately gave them a relative advantage when acclimating to rapid changes. Persecution often spurred them to act. Jewish emigration to America was hastened by the pogroms in Eastern Europe and Russia, and the establishment of the State of Israel was expedited following the Holocaust.[323] In Spain, as well, the pressures from the monarchy led to an unanticipated outcome: as the number of converts increased, so did the Church's suspicions, and as its suspicions grew, so did the demand to expel all the Jews. And when they were expelled pursuant to an edict issued by King Ferdinand and Queen Isabella—which the Jews rightly viewed as a tragedy—it also opened the door to new futures for some of them, in Italy and Morocco, in France and Germany.[324]

And that new future looked like this: nearly three hundred years elapsed between the pogroms of the late fourteenth century and the Theological-Political Treatise written by the pioneering thinker Baruch Spinoza.[325] Three hundred years, but the two events are linked: the Jew whose family had been forced to leave one place ignited a revolution in another. Spinoza was born in 1632 into a Jewish family of *conversos* who, after their expulsion from Spain, lived in the vibrant city of Amsterdam.[326] His revolutionary ideas became milestones in the history of human thinking and also in the history of the Jewish people, and some of those ideas undermined the accepted religious conception of world history.

Spinoza was excommunicated by the Jewish community after spreading heretical ideas. But that didn't prevent him from using his people's history to illustrate his theories. He was ahead of his time and ahead of many generations of contemporary thinkers and historians when he suggested that the survival of the Jews following the destruction of the Temple and years of exile did not derive from divine providence, "but rather from natural, sociological and psychological causes."[327] Something in their collective culture and life circumstances enabled the Jews to continue existing as a distinct entity. It wasn't the God of the Jews who watched over them so they would observe his Torah—rather, it was the Jews who managed to survive and could therefore safeguard God's Torah.

Various historians have chosen to highlight different factors when analyzing the Jewish people and their ability to overcome each of the challenges they faced. But multiple motifs repeat themselves and are often reflected in Jewish rituals, which contributed to their resilience.

That was the case when it came to obvious matters, such as dietary laws that prevented Jews, even in a small and isolated community like the one in India, from mingling with non-Jews.[328] Circumcision also created a clear physical buffer between Jews and non-Jews (with regard to circumcision, Spinoza wrote that "by itself it had the power to preserve their nation forever").[329] It was also true in less obvious matters, such as the requirement to have a quorum of ten men—a *minyan*—for conducting communal religious worship, which compelled the Jews to live in communities of a minimum size and prevented Judaism from becoming a religion of individuals.[330] It was also evident in the formulation of principles such as social justice and mutual responsibility, which served as the glue needed by the community to persuade its members to remain part of it and not opt to leave. Backed by geographical dispersion, insistence on preserving identity, ability to display ideological flexibility, and isolation arising from the suspicions of the surrounding world, the Jews created a set of laws for themselves that enabled them to maintain their solidarity and distinctiveness in the places they ended up in, voluntarily or involuntarily.

What remains from all of this in the twenty-first century? Apart from satisfying one's curiosity, an attempt to uncover the secrets underlying the survival of the Jewish people could determine whether the Jews will manage to survive into the future.

If it's a matter of chance, it won't necessarily continue or necessarily end.

If it's a matter of divine providence, there's no special reason to assume that it will end now, of all times.

However, if the resilience of the Jewish people is the outcome of certain circumstances, if those circumstances still exist, is the toolbox that facilitated Jewish survival still valid?

Jewish law and communal way of life are no longer relevant. Most Jews don't practice daily Jewish rituals. Most Jews don't eat exclusively in Jewish homes or drink wine made exclusively by Jews. Most don't adhere to the directives of a rabbinical leadership with shared principles and values. The non-Jewish surroundings have also changed. Jew-hatred has not disappeared; in fact, it has yet again proved to be resilient. Still, in most countries where Jews live, antisemitism is not an officially legitimized ideology, and its menacing presence is under control. There are many places where Jews are genuinely accepted and connected, at least for now.

Consequently, many social and religious barriers that prevented integration and assimilation don't exist anymore. Jews intermingle with the other groups. They start families comprised of Jews and non-Jews, some of which are Jewish, but most of which are less Jewish.[331] They have difficulty maintaining institutions and traditions whose strength ensures that Judaism will be imparted to the next generation.

Only two communities have managed to avoid that fate: Jews who still practice an active Jewish way of life, and Jews who live in Israel, whose contact with the non-Jewish world is limited by geography. Both those communities also have inherent weaknesses: observant Jews are a minority, and in a world that's becoming increasingly secular, it's doubtful whether they will be the ones creating the Jewish ethos that appeals to the next generation. Israel is a factor whose dominance threatens the continued existence of a global network of Jewish communities. The resilience of the Jewish people used to depend on Diasporic dispersion, but today Israel focuses on political concentration.

In light of the above, can one confidently say that Jews will be around for another two thousand years?

The Jewish ability to acclimate to history's upheavals is remarkable. It required submission to the zeitgeist by those who believed in the values of the past and humility by those who embraced the zeitgeist as opposed to the values of the past. Sustaining the ability to acclimate relies on a distinctive Jewish tradition that facilitates confrontation, debate, and differences of opinion. It's a tradition that insists that "these and these are the words of the living God," as the Talmud says about the teachings of the ideologically opposed talmudic schools of thought, House of Shammai and House of Hillel.[332] It's a tradition that continuously paves alternative paths for Jews to take when needed. It's a tradition found in a constant state of investigation, in a state of self-examination. "The endless quarrels and disputes are the engine…the elixir…If the perpetual ability to argue is taken away from us—that will be our demise," wrote the historian Yehuda Bauer.[333]

So for those who need it, there's room for optimism. Because one thing is clear: Although many tools have disappeared from the Jewish survival kit, it appears that the capacity to quarrel is still very much with us.

HOW DO THE JEWS SURVIVE?

There is no reason: It's a matter of chance that the Jews have survived for so many years.

A religious reason:

- Jewish: God watches over the Jews, the chosen people.
- Non-Jewish: God protects the Jews as proof of the victory of Christianity.

Structural reasons: (a partial list, the reasons are intertwined):

- They contributed to society at large, which generally protected them.
- The belief in a "chosen people" preserved an awareness that necessitates distinct continuity.

- The transition to life according to Jewish law (halakha) made it possible to be a people without a country.
- The Jews' dispersion enabled Judaism to persist even in the face of large-scale disasters.
- The culture of argument and debate added a dimension of ideological flexibility and an ability to acclimate.
- The emphasis on literacy and education prepared the Jews for coping with changes.
- Cultural autonomy and antisemitism were unifying factors that prevented assimilation.

Question 6:

Israel or Diaspora?

"As a result of the historic catastrophe in which Titus of Rome destroyed Jerusalem and Israel was exiled from its land, I was born in one of the cities of the Exile. But always I regarded myself as one who was born in Jerusalem." (Shmuel Yosef (Shai) Agnon, excerpts from his Nobel Prize acceptance speech)[334]

Four thousand six hundred eighty-two years after the creation of the world according to Jewish tradition, in the year 922 AD, Jews assembled to celebrate the Seder night on two different days.[335] In the Land of Israel, Passover began on a Sunday, whereas in Babylonia, the Jews gathered to mark the exodus from Egypt only on Tuesday of that week. When the Jews in Israel had already asked the Four Questions, the Jews in Babylonia were still preparing for the holiday by burning the leavened foods they had found. When the Jews in Babylonia were still drinking the four glasses of wine, the Jews in Israel were in the middle of *Chol Hamoed*—the intermediate festival days.[336] Two major Jewish communities—two different calendars, and not only for one particular holiday, but for a number of holidays, and perhaps for a number of years. Not all of the details regarding that event are known to us.

This is an early example of an acute crisis in Israel-Diaspora relations—a crisis whose manifestations can also be seen in other crises, from then until now. Ever since Jews were exiled from their land and began building vibrant communities in other places, a persistent tension has existed in the Jewish world regarding Israel's role—once the Land of Israel, and now the State of Israel. Is Israel the place where all Jews are supposed to gather together, or is it merely a place one yearns for, with no real need to spend time there? Is what takes place in Israel more important than what happens in other communities in the Jewish world, or can Jews only fulfill their destiny when dispersed? Is the State of Israel a current metamorphosis on the path to religious or secular-political redemption, or a digression from Judaism's high road of living as a global people?

Theoretical and actual inner conflicts regarding the role of Israel as a place and a community are not new to Judaism. They emerged as early as the Babylonians' conquest of the Kingdom of Judah in 604 BC. They existed when groups of exiles returned to the Land of Israel in the days of Ezra the Scribe (and most Jews remained elsewhere). The conflicted Jewish relationship with Israel is present in Alexandria when the Jewish community grew after Alexander the Great's conquests and the Roman conquest, during the building of Herod's Temple and its subsequent destruction, the rebellion, and the Exile.

In the period when the Land of Israel was under Muslim rule, from 638 AD to the end of the eleventh century, Jews were allowed to return to the country. The bond between the Jews living in the Land of Israel and those in the Diaspora became stronger.[337] The drama of great schism over the Jewish calendar occurred during this period. Two eminent Jews played the leading roles: Saadia Gaon of Sura, Babylonia, and Aharon Ben Meir, who lived in Tiberias in the Land of Israel.[338] The discovery of the Cairo Genizah in the nineteenth century revealed previously unknown details about the battle between these two men, which divided Jew from Jew, date from date, and holiday from holiday.

The exact reason for the dispute is complicated and somewhat esoteric. It concerns the procedure used by Jews to precisely calculate the lunar conjunction, which is the moment that determines the start of a new month and the consequent fixing of the Jewish calendar and festivals.[339] But like many other differences of opinion between Jews, the critical question that Saadia Gaon and Ben Meir bickered over was not how to calculate the calendar, but who was authorized to decide which method would be employed. It was a debate over authority.

Nearly six hundred years before this pair of scholars quarreled, a decision had been made that the Jewish calendar would be fixed using a mathematical calculation of the moon's phases and not based on an ancient tradition that required witnesses to testify before a court that they had observed the lunar conjunction. Ben Meir believed, however, that one key element of the old tradition had to be preserved—namely, that the calendar must remain under the jurisdiction of the rabbinic authorities in the Land of Israel. And in practical terms, it meant that he, Ben Meir, was the one to decide.

That argument was rejected by Saadia Gaon, especially that year because, at least according to him, Ben Meir had erred in his calculation. "You set the calendar according to your custom, and we also follow the custom of our fathers and we set the calendar in our own way," wrote Gaon in a forceful letter.[340] The Jews in Babylonia considered themselves just as much the leading community of the Jewish world as those who lived in Israel, owing to their accomplishments and abilities. Granted, the community in Israel could flaunt their geographical advantage—living in the Promised Land—which was also the ancient and exclusive seat of the Sanhedrin, the highest court of justice and the supreme council in ancient Jerusalem. But the Babylonian community claimed that after King Jehoiachin of Judah was exiled and founded a *yeshiva* in Babylonia, the absolute authority rested with them until redemption would be attained.[341,342]

Israel versus the Diaspora: who leads, who decides? Which is the preferred place to live? Today's disputes are dressed in yesterday's garb.

The State of Israel's Proclamation of Independence starts as follows: "The Land of Israel was the birthplace of the Jewish people. Here, their spiritual, religious, and political identity was shaped."[343] That description is not consistent with the Jewish story. What made the Jews distinct, as opposed to other peoples, is that the Jewish nation was not born in its own country, but on a journey to it.[344,345] The nation's forefathers, Abraham and Jacob, had journeyed between Haran and Canaan, Aram and Egypt. The same holds true for their descendants, who became a people in Egypt and received the Torah while wandering in the desert. Although the biblical story grants the Jewish people the right to settle in the Land of Israel, it is also careful to mention that the land doesn't belong to them.[346,347]

The bulk of the formative events in Jewish history did not occur in the Land of Israel. The Jews always considered Israel their land, but most of the time (including today) lived in other places.[348,349] Consequently, throughout the Jewish timeline, most of the issues relating to the Land of Israel were discussed from the perspective of deportees, exiles, yearners, and wanderers. Jews could debate—from a distance—about when and how the Redemption would come and how the world would look afterward. They could debate about whether the Exile is the crime or its punishment. They could wonder whether the Jews would ever return to their land and be the masters of their fate.

The upheavals of the nineteenth and twentieth centuries undermined the validity of most of those debates. Many Jews stopped taking an interest in questions of theological crime and punishment. Some were persuaded to return to their land in an attempt to be masters of their own fate — a position that Jews were not used to and had achieved, to some degree, only twice before: in the tenth century BCE in the days of David and Solomon, and in the first and second centuries BCE, in the days of the Hasmonean Kingdom.[350,351] Such a position invalidates the understanding of Jewish time as extending between two poles: Exile and the Redemption. It would necessitate a reevaluation of Jewish time that's neither.[352]

In a book he wrote shortly after the State of Israel was founded, Arthur Koestler maintained that its establishment was sufficient grounds for Jews to choose one of two options: "return to the Promised Land, or recognize that that faith is no longer theirs," meaning, remain in the Diaspora and assimilate. The "Wandering Jew" is no longer necessary, he wrote. "His mission is completed."[353]

Is it beneficial to the Jews that they now have a political national framework, or is it preferable to cling to the culture shaped by the thousands of years spent as a people dispersed among other nations? Put differently, is there a Jewish culture worth sustaining in a national framework, and if there is, what form should it take? Or has Judaism, over the long years of exile, assumed a new purpose adapted to the conditions of dispersion that history forced on it, to which it is better suited?

That question led to a fiery debate in the early days of Zionism.[354] Some favored the Israel-sovereignty option as a way to provide a refuge against Jew-hatred (Theodor Herzl). Others viewed the Land of Israel as a refuge primarily against spiritual assimilation (Ahad Ha'am). Many others saw no need for the Zionist idea and preferred to strengthen the Jewish communities in the Diaspora (Simon Dubnow)[355] or even bitterly opposed it (Hermann Cohen).[356] A few of the objectors to a national Jewish framework relied in their reasoning on survival considerations (being dispersed is better than being concentrated in a single place)—an explanation that is frequently voiced in the nuclear age[357]—while others relied on substantive reasons (the Jews have a mission which they can fulfill only if dispersed among other peoples).[358]

Is it good for the Jews to live separately, or is it better for them to live among other people? Does Judaism benefit when Jews live separately, or is Judaism at its best when Jews live dispersed among other people? Those questions have a practical dimension: where will the Jews manage to exist and thrive? Those questions also have a principled dimension: where should Jews aspire to exist and thrive? Herzl—a journalist, playwright, and statesman—wanted a Jewish state due to practical considerations, having lost faith in the Emancipation.[359] Hermann Cohen, a philosopher, wanted to sustain Jewish existence in the Diaspora due to principled considerations—he believed that Judaism has a pivotal role to play in repairing humanity, which justifies abandoning the aspiration for distinct Jewish sovereignty in the Land of Israel.[360,361]

After King Cyrus allowed the Jews in Babylonia to return to the Land of Israel, most chose to remain in exile. They may have missed their land, but their longing didn't include a deep desire to settle there again.[362] According to Arthur Hertzberg, a twentieth-century Jewish American rabbi and thinker, "the character of the Jews is of sophisticated nomads." They love their homeland passionately, but at the same time are also the "most cosmopolitan people."[363]

What role does the State of Israel play in the life of a cosmopolitan people?

In its early days, Zionism had an answer to that question: to rescue the Jews and Judaism from their situation and put an end to cosmopolitanism. The historian Ben-Zion Dinur expressed that insight without mincing words: "There's one problem with Judaism, and it is called exile."[364] Political Zionism stressed the need to offer the Jews a physical refuge from antisemitism. Its adherents had woken up from the dream of integrating with other nations and believed that only a defined and secure geographic territory could sustain the Jews. On the other hand, spiritual Zionism emphasized the need to offer the Jews a cultural refuge from assimilation. Its adherents realized that the prospect of preserving Judaism when among other nations wasn't viable. They believed that only a defined geographic territory could supply Judaism with the spiritual energy for its continued existence. In other words, political Zionism wanted to rescue the Jews from the dangers threatening them from the outside, whereas spiritual Zionism wanted to rescue the Jews from the dangers threatening them from the inside. Both of them assumed that the product of their actions would be a "new" Jew.[365] They understood that Jewish emigration to the Land of Israel was not just another move to a new house but a turnabout in Jewish consciousness.

And the Jewish state did transform the Jewish reality. It concentrated a large group of people in one place, from Europe, North Africa, and other parts of the world, who are likely to become the majority of the Jewish people at some point in the near future.[366] Israel revived an ancient language and gave impetus to the renaissance of a distinct Jewish culture. Israel has considerable organized strength to take action, which was unparalleled in the Jewish world and almost certainly never existed before; Israel offers a paradigm for life where being Jewish is the convenient default.[367] In other words, the Jewish state changed the Jews' consciousness. But to be more exact, it changed the consciousness of the Jews living in Israel in one way and the consciousness of the Jews living outside Israel in another.

That disparity between the two types of change has, on occasion, taken the form of tension between Jews in Israel and Jews in other countries.[368] It occurs when the Israeli government finds itself at odds with the government of another country where many Jews live. It occurs when Israel urges Jews from other countries to emigrate, making them suspect in the eyes of their neighbors. It occurs when Israel expects Jews living in other places to support its policies and try to persuade their countries to do so as well. It occurs when the Israeli government adopts a policy which the majority of Jews in the Diaspora object to. In other words, for Jews in the Diaspora, Israel is at times a source of pride, and at times a burden.[369]

The Zionism that Israelis embrace assumes that Israel is the only place where Jewish life can be fully expressed.[370] It's a modern secular version of an old religious assertion, which some of the greatest Jewish scholars subscribed to in the past.[371] According to Nachmanides, one of the leading sages in Spain in the thirteenth century, the Commandments only have genuine value when fulfilled in the Land of Israel. The Commandments should be fulfilled in the Diaspora only so they won't be forgotten, and so they won't be lost. But intrinsically, they are required only in the Land of Israel.[372,373] Although David Ben-Gurion wasn't particularly interested in observing all the Mitzvot, he, too, accepted the premise that only Israel gives meaning to the observance of Jewish life, and wrote: "There is no Jew in the Diaspora…who can be a complete Jew, and there is no Jewish community in the Diaspora that is able to live a complete Jewish life. Only in the State of Israel is a complete Jewish life possible."[374]

Ben-Gurion was deeply familiar with Jewish history. He believed there's a hierarchy between important periods characterized by sovereignty and insignificant periods where the Jews lacked sovereignty. Many of his colleagues in the Zionist movement shared that view. The socialist-Zionist ideologue Nahman Sirkin wrote that "only in the modern period has Judaism come back to life." For him, "Judaism of the Middle Ages," "religious Judaism," and "Judaism of the Diaspora" were antithetical to the Judaism that had been revived.[375] Put differently, the greater part of Jewish history is the history of a Judaism that is lifeless. The Israeli novelist A. B. Yehoshua expressed similar views in more recent years. He believed there is Jewish meaning in everything a Jew living in Israel does, as opposed to life in the Diaspora, where the Jew wears his Jewish identity only on occasion and not all the time. Yehoshua's remarks caused an outcry in the Diaspora, who didn't like hearing that their Judaism was less meaningful than his.[376,377]

But in contrast to Israeli Zionism, which for many years made itself the main focus, there have been, and still are, other approaches. For instance, there's a minority approach that posits that Israel is an intrusion that makes it more difficult for the Jews to continue practicing a way of life that's right for them as a cosmopolitan people. Take, for example, the brothers Daniel and Jonathan Boyarin, contemporary, non-Zionist American Jewish scholars, who maintain that "confining Judaism to a state generates a complete change in the meanings of the Jews' lifestyles and social behavior patterns."[378,379]

For some time now, the majority of Jews have accepted Zionism.[380] The old Zionist version that did not accept the legitimacy of Diasporic Jewish existence is somewhat out of fashion, and this makes Zionism more digestible to all Jews in a form that contends that fortifying the Diaspora is one of Zionism's roles.[381] That's what the American rabbi and avant-garde thinker Mordecai Kaplan believed. Kaplan argued that following the establishment of the State of Israel, the purpose of Zionism is to help safeguard the identity of the Jewish people wherever Jews reside.[382] "The upbuilding of the Land of Israel is a necessary condition for the renaissance of Jewish life in the Diaspora," Kaplan wrote.[383] Many agreed with him, including, for instance, the American Zionist leader, Abba Hillel Silver.[384]

Silver played an important role in the Zionist enterprise that led to the establishment of the State of Israel.[385] But after the State was established, he soon lost the ability to influence how it was being shaped due to a bitter struggle with Israel's leaders, particularly Ben-Gurion.[386]

The debate was over power and influence but also an ideological contest of at least equal magnitude.[387] Similar to Hermann Cohen, Silver felt that Judaism had a role to play in repairing the world. That role, he believed, could not be accomplished by the Jews as long as they were preoccupied with a battle for survival when faced with antisemitism and threats of annihilation. However, the establishment of a new state, which heals the

"the defensive Diaspora Jewish mentality," would also engender a new Jew—a new Zionist-Israeli Jew and, at the same time, a new Zionist-Diaspora Jew.[388] It's not surprising that this new Zionist-Diaspora Jew emerged not only after the founding of an autonomous Jewish state but also in the place where Jews could lead an undisturbed Jewish life—in America. The American Jew, who lives in a Diaspora free from persecution, could look with pride at the homeland he doesn't live in and draw strength from it as it helps him "march forward in fulfilling the missions intended for us as the People of the Covenant."[389]And next to that Jew who lives in comfort, the Israeli Jew can also unwind.

Although the negation of the Diaspora has not disappeared from the Israeli landscape, it's less dominant. Some have even abandoned that position, claiming it's no longer relevant.[390] That is because Israel is a stronger country today, surer of itself and its standing. It also stems from the recognition that for many people (Jews and non-Jews alike), a twenty-first-century lifestyle often means moving and relocating at some point in their lifetime or having more than one address at the same time.

For many generations, Jews wrestled with the following question: Should the Jewish people wait for redemption and the Messiah before returning to their land—meaning, maybe never—or is it preferable to return to their land before the Redemption comes, thereby even expediting it? The philosopher and liturgist Judah Halevi, whose poems about yearning for Zion are still heart-wrenching today, addressed that dilemma in his book, *The Kuzari*. Should Jews, he wrote, make peace with the Diaspora or consider it vile?[391] His dramatic and ultimately tragic decision to set out on a journey to the Land of Israel, during which he met his death, did not fully resolve his question: perhaps he embarked on that perilous journey as a personal act that articulated his longings for the distant land; or perhaps he viewed it as an act that was national, whose purpose was to hasten the coming of the Redemption.[392,393]

Either way, the change in circumstances since the earlier days of Zionism at the end of the 19th century has taken some of the sting out of the Exile-Redemption, Zion-Diaspora dilemmas. Of course, the fierce and prolonged war that engulfed Israel, following the October 7, 2023 massacre was a psychological shock, so dramatic that some Jews even wondered about the long-term feasibility of the political Jewish enterprise in the Middle East. Still, most Jews—those who subscribe to the Zionist idea as the healthy manifestation of the Jewish condition and also those who still oppose it—agree that Israel is currently the major player in the contemporary Jewish world.[394] In other words, even if the theoretical debate about whether statehood is good for Judaism remains up in the air, it has been decided—at least for now—in the real world.[395]

ISRAEL'S ROLE: DISPUTED POSSIBILITIES

1. The Land of Israel and/or the State of Israel is *the only place* where a full Jewish life can be observed (in its religious or its secular-cultural version).
2. Israel is *the leading community* of the Jewish people *by virtue of intrinsic preference* (and according to the religious version, perhaps as part of the redemption process).
3. Israel is the leading community of the Jewish people *by virtue of the circumstances* (organized strength, numbers, etc.).
4. Israel is one of many important Jewish communities.
5. Jewish sovereignty in Israel will be achieved *only with the coming of the Redemption.*
6. Jews are a diasporic people, and there is an *intrinsic preference for dispersion* over their concentration in Israel.

Question 7:

Jewish Genius—Does It Exist?

"Yes, I am a Jew, and when the ancestors of the right honorable gentleman were brutal savages in an unknown island, mine were priests in the temple of Solomon."
(Benjamin Disraeli)[396]

Here's a short story about Jewish genius, and about Jewish loyalty, and also—no less important—about Jewish humor. It begins with a telegram sent from London to the celebrated physicist Albert Einstein, who was in Berlin at the time. The sender was also a scientist and a biochemist, whose name was Chaim Weizmann. And he had a request: that Einstein accompany him on a trip to America to raise money for Jewish settlement in Palestine and establish a Hebrew university.

At first, Einstein wasn't particularly eager to join the mission, but after some persuasion, he relented. He wrote to his publisher in France, "I am not keen on going to America but am just doing it on behalf of the Zionists."[397] Together with

Weizmann, Einstein and his wife, Elsa, crossed the Atlantic in March 1921.

As soon as they set sail, the physicist wanted to make sure that Weizmann understood the theory of relativity, which Einstein had published a few years earlier. He wasn't reassured about the biochemist's mastery of the theory. Or at least one can surmise such a conclusion from what transpired between the two men according to the account Weizmann provided at the end of the journey: "Einstein," Weizmann recounted, "explained his theory to me every day. When we reached our destination, I was convinced, beyond any doubt, that he really understood it."

Einstein felt distant from the Jewish faith but considered himself a Jew in the sense of "nationality and origin," as he tersely wrote to the rabbis of Berlin. The more Einstein insisted on underscoring his Jewishness, the more of a symbol he became—even among Jews who didn't come close to comprehending his worldview. "Among famous Jews, Einstein is in a category unto himself," Steven Gimbel wrote in his book *Einstein's Jewish Science*.[398] Gimbel starts the book with one of the best quotes from the eminent scientist, taken from a speech Einstein delivered in France in April 1922: "If my theory of relativity is proven successful, Germany will claim me as a German and France will declare me a citizen of the world. Should my theory prove untrue, France will say that I am a German and Germany will declare that I am a Jew."[399]

It's unfortunate that Voltaire, the renowned French philosopher who published a venomous article against the Jews nearly 150 years prior to Einstein's speech, didn't get to meet the eminent Jew in Paris and have a taste of his biting wit. Voltaire believed that the Jews made no significant contribution to the world. He said they are "an ignorant and barbarous people," and surpass other nations only "in impertinent fables and bad conduct."[400] Voltaire never met Einstein, nor the psychoanalyst Sigmund Freud or the writer Franz Kafka. "From Irving Berlin to Isaiah Berlin,"[401] Jews who revolutionized the foundations of Western thought and culture in the last few centuries—composers and philosophers, writers and artists, scientists and musicians.

Nearly everyone who has spoken or written about the Jewish contribution to the world opens with a list of names or achievements that prove how Jewish excellence has benefited the greater good. About a fifth of all Nobel Prize laureates are Jewish, one hundred times more than the Jewish share of the global population.[402] Furthermore, 42 percent of the authors of the fifty most-quoted books in the twentieth century are Jewish. Over 50 percent of the world chess champions have had at least one Jewish parent.[403] A quarter of the recipients of the Turing Award in Computer Science are Jewish, and nearly one-third of all the Fields Medal winners awarded by the International Mathematical Union are Jewish. Add to that the pivotal role that Jews have played in developing the American film industry, their prominence as comedians and humor artists (primarily in the United States), their representation in the upper echelons of the global hi-tech industry—whether as individual entrepreneurs or thanks to being part of "the startup nation"[404]—and their proven ability in banking and investments.[405]

It's hard to deny, at least in modern times, that Jews excel well beyond what one would expect, given their small size in proportion to the global population.[406] It's hard to deny that they stand out in their contribution to society. But two questions remain unanswered: When did they start excelling? And why?

The spread of monotheism, the formation of the Bible, and the innovative debates about Oral Law all took place in an early Jewish era. Judaism's far-reaching impact on the world has been evident since then: Christianity emerged from Judaism, and Judaism also had a clear influence on Islam.[407] In the interim, the Talmud's erudite teachings and commentaries took shape and are still compelling proof of the Jews' time-honored wisdom, even in the eyes of those who have never met a Jew. (The stories about the Talmud's impact in South Korea can testify to that).[408]

When did the Jews start excelling? Although they produced a unique work in the embryonic stages of their history, it appears that excellence of the variety we're familiar with today first emerged at the beginning of the first millennium AD. The key to that process was literacy. Its origins can be traced to the Torah's Commandments ("and you shall teach them to your sons"), but later sources suggest that Jews stressed the importance of learning. "The law does not permit to make festivals at the births of our children, and thereby afford occasion of drinking to excess...but it commands us to bring those children up in learning." Those words were written by Flavius Josephus when describing the customs of the Jews at the end of the first century AD.[409]

Not all Jews adhered to that dictate. Nonetheless, the gradual course of history turned it into a permanent, stable and significant element of Judaism.[410] It began with the victory of the Pharisees—a faction that stressed the study of the Torah—over the Sadducees, who favored priestly rituals. (Actually, it was the Romans who prevailed over the Sadducees, and the Pharisees were the ones who survived.)[411] As time elapsed and Judaism became increasingly identified with education, people who took no interest in learning or were not inclined to study gradually left its ranks.[412] In the process, the Jewish people lost up to two-thirds of its members—resulting in a sharp decline from 4.5 million in the first century AD to only 1.5 million in the eighth century. But some scholars believe it also explains how the Jews became a literate people who transitioned naturally from being farmers to working in occupations requiring education, reading, and writing. According to a research study dealing with the twelfth and thirteenth centuries, the subsequent outcome of that transition was a multiplicity of Jewish scientists as early as the beginning of the second millennium AD.[413]

Other historical developments, including restrictions that were imposed on the Jews, led them to focus their vocations even more. Because they could not own land, they were forced to make a living from businesses that didn't require a brick-and-mortar presence. Because their religion enabled them to charge interest on loans, they turned to money lending and related financial occupations—bookkeeping, reading and writing promissory notes, and litigation.[414] As they were persecuted and compelled to move from place to place, the Jews became accustomed to transferring capital. Their ability to communicate, common culture, and dispersion around the world were all tools that gave Jews an advantage over others in promoting international trade. "Know that wherever there is money, there are Jews," asserted the French philosopher Charles-Louis Montesquieu—a rather malicious description considering it was written in the middle of the eighteenth century, when most Jews were living in abject poverty.[415] But Montesquieu had respect for what the Jews managed to achieve. He credited them with the development of modern international trade due to their persecution and the means they devised to defend themselves against it.[416]

So we have two possible explanations for Jewish excellence: One attributes it primarily to endogenous Jewish factors, to the emphasis placed on the value of learning and education. The other attributes Jewish excellence to exogenous factors—the Jews were prodded/forced into certain occupations and industries, which over time positioned them at the forefront of many human endeavors. Trends associated with both these categories—political, social, and economic—have impacted the unavoidable interplay between Jews and the non-Jewish world. Therefore, most explanations for Jewish excellence—combined with the eternal explanation of divine providence—fall into these two categories.[417]

But not all of them.

There's one explanation that doesn't necessarily belong to the endogenous category (what the Jews did) or to the exogenous one (what was done to the Jews). It's an explanation that has nothing to do with how people conduct themselves but rather to do with their biology. It's an explanation that should be approached with caution and with reservations. We briefly and hesitatingly touch on the issue of the "Jewish gene"—does it exist or not—because it's out there and avoiding it completely would be dishonest.

It's a discussion that generates intense and justifiable feelings of discomfort—because Jewishness that has a hereditary dimension is Jewishness that has racial overtones. And as has been proven in the past, that kind of Jewishness puts Jews at risk.[418]

It's a discussion whose backdrop contains a fair measure of ideology—political contexts that pertain, for example, to the Jewish connection with the Land of Israel.

It's a discussion that has a specific, professional component and is held among geneticists, which most Jews—despite how smart they are—are not qualified to understand in any depth.

More genetic research studies have been conducted about Jews than any other religious or ethnic group.[419] The interest in them is, first and foremost, medical and has applied implications. Some Jews "are at much greater risk of developing certain genetic disorders or illnesses impacted by genetics, relative to the majority of the population in the countries they live in."

But the broader, historical context of Jewish genetics cannot be evaded.

A well-known research study posited that the members of the Jewish priestly class (*kohanim)* can for the most part trace their lineage to a common ancestor[420] who most likely lived in the biblical period when Jewish history was first recorded, and caused a predictable stir. Naturally, there was some criticism as well.[421] Later studies that identified a "shared Middle Eastern ancestry" among all Jews—Moroccans and Ashkenazis, Turks and Iranians, Syrians and Italians[422]—also produced excitement and even greater controversies.[423] A shared Middle Eastern ancestry seemingly supports a political claim that is a pillar of Zionism—namely, that the Jews did, in fact, return to their homeland and didn't merely conquer territory belonging to someone else. It's therefore not surprising that the debates over research with such findings are ongoing today.[424]

These research studies ostensibly prove that Jews share a common ancestry. That's a fascinating finding. In this chapter, however, we're concerned with a much more focused contention: that Jews are of particularly high intelligence and that, as the British scientist Charles Percy Snow suggested, "there is something in the Jewish gene pool that produces talent."[425] If certain genetic diseases are more common among Jews, why shouldn't they be carriers of other genetic traits as well, such as intelligence? One of the most quoted studies dealing with Jewish intelligence—a study so controversial that *The New York Times* considered it illegitimate to quote[426]—claims just that and even more:[427] the Jews who were studied had "a higher IQ than any other ethnic group." Particular genetic disorders (Tay-Sachs disease, Gaucher disease, Niemann-Pick disease) are more prevalent among Jews, and so is intelligence.[428]

Whether Jews are truly smarter than other groups is open to debate. One research study ranked them high on the list, whereas a different one lowered the bar a bit.[429] There are also numerous theories about how they became—if indeed they became—hereditarily smarter than other groups of people. Intelligence is a trait that has a hereditary component. Maybe the Jews have an abundance of it, maybe not. Perhaps they'll continue passing it on to their offspring. Maybe the high share of intermarriages makes all future hereditary arguments obsolete.

There's no need to choose between scientific, cultural, and environmental explanations for Jewish prominence in science and the arts, philosophy, and technology. And, as Jon Entine put it, there's no need to choose between the influence of "Jewish mothers" and the influence of "Jewish genes."[430] Freud believed that racial differences exist between Jews and non-Jews and that Jewish culture advanced the capacity for abstraction among those who adhered to it.[431] In other words, he believed both in genes and in culture. Multiple factors contributed to the process that catapulted the Jews to where they are.

And perhaps the most crucial one was the window of opportunity that history opened, the window of opportunity that the modern era opened. "For the descendants of Philo and Maimonides, the rationalistic movement of the eighteenth century was in part a repetition of a well-known historical process," wrote the historian Dubnow.[432] The Jews were an educated minority, and doors suddenly opened up for them. They were a devitalized minority looking for a way to stand out and gain strength. They were a discriminated minority for whom a relatively neutral domain like science was a natural arena. They were an excluded minority, and it was the cracks in the wall through which they squeezed that offered an unexpected and endless sea of possibilities. They had been preparing for the opportune moment to forge ahead for many years, and suddenly it arrived.

In his book *The Jewish Century*, the historian Yuri Slezkine posits that the "modern age is the Jewish age."[433] The initial premise he presents is that modernization means that everyone wants to be "urban, mobile, literate, articulate, intellectually intricate, physically fastidious, and occupationally flexible." Modernization is about "pursuing wealth for the sake of learning, learning for the sake of wealth, and both wealth and learning for their own sake." Modernization, in other words, is about "everyone becoming Jewish."

And who, of course, is better at being Jewish "than the Jews themselves." It was Jews like Einstein who seized the moment that history had placed on their doorstep.

When Einstein began his research in theoretical physics, he entered a wasteland that only a select few took an interest in. After he began disseminating his ideas, another renowned physicist, Arnold Sommerfeld, wrote that there was something "almost unhealthy" about them, which reflects the "abstract-conceptual character of the Semite."[434] Sommerfeld later became Einstein's friend and defender, as well as the defender of other Jewish scientists in Germany's darkest hour. To his credit, it didn't take him long to acknowledge that a revolutionary, novel, and undisputed theory had emerged from Einstein's capacity for abstraction and generalization. Also to his credit, he rightly identified that Einstein's scientific breakthrough embodied something "peculiarly Jewish," as the historian Paul Johnson defined it. Jewish—because of the capacity for abstraction and the need for generalization. Jewish—because "it was impelled by an overwhelming need for an enveloping truth-law about the universe, a scientific Torah."[435]

It's hard to say with certainty where the Jews get that need from. But it's interesting to note that many of the Jews who today are considered proof of Jewish genius came from assimilated homes, and some even from families of apostates. Those Jews didn't view their Judaism as something crucial to their work. Karl Marx's prominence cannot be attributed to "Jewish" education in its simplest form, but what about to his sensitivity to social justice? The revolutionary composer Arnold Schoenberg converted to Christianity before reconverting to Judaism (at a ceremony whose witnesses were Einstein's son-in-law and the artist Marc Chagall).[436] The genius of Benjamin Disraeli, Britain's legendary prime minister, was shaped in a family that chose to have their children baptized.

Disraeli's biographer, Robert Blake, attaches minor importance to the eminent statesman's Jewishness (although he doesn't spare Disraeli from a seemingly antisemitic insult concerning his "certainly un-Jewish" financial incompetence).[437] For Blake, like other historians, the Jewish ingredient was no more than a "digression" from the main story.[438] Some disagree, both in Disraeli's case and in the case of other accomplished Jews, such as the author Franz Kafka—whose Jewishness seems almost trivial to some of his literary critics, whereas others believe it had tremendous impact.[439]

And it needs to be said: In many instances, the Jews are notably the ones who tend to attach considerable significance to the Jewishness of distinguished Jews.[440] They are also the ones who usually provide corroborating evidence. With regard to Disraeli, their proof would be the fact that the great statesman continued to regard himself as a Jew (in the racial sense).

Furthermore, many of his non-Jewish contemporaries also considered him a Jew ("The old Jew, he is the man," was how Otto von Bismarck referred to him at the Congress of Berlin),[441] even though Disraeli never chose to be a Jew again (in the religious sense). All this made it easier for Jews to continue associating Disraeli with themselves, with their culture, and with the growing list of Jews who have made a meaningful contribution to the advancement of human society.

The Jewish British historian Cecil Roth also published a biography of Disraeli. Its original title in English was *Disraeli, Earl of Beaconsfield*, whereas the Hebrew translation is called *Disraeli the Jew*.[442]

Why did the Hebrew translation add the word "Jew" to the title? One can speculate about the answer based on another book that Roth wrote, *The Jewish Contribution to Civilization*.[443] In the latter, Roth offers an interesting justification for why Jews who are no longer Jewish should be included in the list of those who made an important contribution to mankind—a justification which is no doubt a product of the year the book was published in—1938, on the eve of the Second World War.

The assault on the Jews is racial in nature, Roth maintained. They are racial in the sense that some Jews are persecuted owing to the actions of non-Jews of Jewish origin, and some non-Jews are persecuted due to their Jewish origin. That being the case, Roth argued the following: "If the Jewish people are to receive a full measure of blame for the one category, it is justified in claiming some measure of credit for the other," including those "whose immediate ancestors professed the Jewish religion." Put simply, because Jew haters count non-Jews of Jewish origin as part of the Jewish nation when it's to our detriment, we'll also count non-Jews of Jewish origin when it's to our advantage.

And when we do count them, we find that among the Jews who made a significant contribution to civilization, many rebelled against their Judaism—whether the religion, the tradition, the people, or the culture, either by act or by omission. We find that a substantial share of the contribution made by Jews to mankind is by those who were conspicuously detached from Jewish society—and that they themselves, or their parents, renounced their Jewish heritage. Judaism may have been a launching pad for them, but on their rise to greatness, revolutions, and breakthroughs, they distanced themselves from Judaism and left it behind.

That's an interesting and perhaps disturbing fact which raises questions about the priorities of Jews in the future.

If Jews strive for excellence, and if abandoning Judaism has on occasion facilitated attaining excellence—does that mean that Jewish genius, coupled with its inherent advantages, is also a kind of sophisticated mechanism of self-destruction?

Or maybe today, when Jews no longer suffer from official discrimination in the major communities they live in nor are they required by their neighbors to disengage from their traditions if they want to get ahead in life, will it be possible to pursue that same excellence without having to abandon Jewish tradition?

WHY DO JEWS EXCEL?

Endogenous factors

Cultural development: Since the early days of Jewish history, Jews have placed emphasis on learning.

Social screening process: There are norms which in practice weeded out the uneducated.

Psychology: A minority mentality drives Jews to stand out and excel in the absence of other assets.

Exogenous factors

Discrimination forced Jews to engage in certain occupations, excluded them from owning land, and impelled them to develop alternatives.

History's contribution: the disappearance of Sadducee Judaism, the type of challenges that evolved in the modern age

Genetics

Genetic bias: Their genes make Jews smart (and for that reason they cultivated a culture of education).

Epilogue:

Does Judaism Have a Future?

"…in the days of the Messiah…the world will follow its normal course."
(Maimonides, Laws of Repentance 9:2)[444]

Why would anyone want to be a Jew?

Alain Elkann is a Jew who was born in the United States in 1950. But his parents, who had emigrated there before the Second World War, took him back to Europe.

They were respected Jews in their community. His father, a native of Alsace, became the president of the Jewish community in Paris. His mother grew up in Torino, Italy, where the young Alain was sent to attend a Jewish school.

He wrote a book about his life, entitled *Mitzva*.[445] The book is about his life as an assimilated Jew who's growing apart from his Judaism but is still trying to hold on to some remnants. He married a Catholic woman, the daughter of the founder and former CEO of Fiat, and their children were baptized. He himself didn't convert to Christianity, even though it would have been "easier" to do so.

So, why not?

"Something deep, a hidden pride, always helped me avoid the temptation, evade the danger," Elkann wrote. But even though he chose to cling to his Judaism, he didn't become an involved Jew. He goes to synagogue once a year, like he did with his father as a child. "To be honest," he writes in his book, "we'd like to close our eyes and think we are Jews just one day a year, on Yom Kippur." The yearly visit to the La Victoire synagogue in Paris helps him remember "who I am and what I was."

Elkann made a choice. His reasons aren't entirely clear. Like him, many Jews have to choose or are able to choose. The world is open to them. So what do they choose?

Sometimes, they choose to vanish like many did before them. Almost every recent book about Jewish history mentions, at least in passing, the bleak statistics about Moses Mendelssohn's family. Mendelssohn, the father of the *Haskalah,* the Jewish Enlightenment movement, was one of the first to confront the challenges faced by Jews in the modern age. He confronted them with courage. He confronted them with wisdom. But the result, as far as the Jewish survival instinct is concerned, was not terribly impressive: his grandchildren were Christian Germans, and most of his offspring abandoned Judaism.[446] And they were not the only ones who renounced their faith. According to the historian Heinrich Graetz, nearly one-half of Berlin's Jewish population converted to Christianity in the days of Mendelssohn.[447] There were 1,236 conversions over a very short period.[448] In earlier periods, many more assimilated, whether by choice or by force.[449]

Leaving the ranks is even easier today than it was during certain periods in the past. The poet Heinrich Heine and many of his contemporaries converted to Christianity due to their desire to acquire a "ticket" to European culture. But today, such a ticket is no longer required, and a utilitarian explanation is less compelling.[450] For most Jews who assimilate, it's a simple transition that occurs seamlessly, devoid of intense drama or unbearable pain. Assimilation no longer comes with a steep social price because most Western societies are tolerant of people who have no pronounced religious or ethnic affiliation. It's not easily detectable because, unlike in the past, Jews can no longer be identified by the way they look, their clothing, or any other distinctive mark. And even better: today's Jew doesn't have to be untrue to himself and feign belief in another religion to stop being Jewish. He doesn't have to convert to Islam or Christianity. Leaving the ranks is a smooth process that primarily takes place among Jews whose level of commitment to Judaism isn't that high.[451] It's almost a casual drift from the Jewish world to the world outside — a drift many Jews have taken.[452] In the United States today, millions of people have a parent, or a parent of a parent, who is considered "Jewish," but they themselves are no longer Jewish.[453]

And, of course, there are those who remain. Some are Jews because of inertia. Their Judaism is a fact of life they saw no need to change. They are children of Jews, so they are Jews.

Some are Jews thanks to personal ties and their surroundings. They have parents, siblings, partners, friends, or a community comprised of Jews (especially if they live in Israel).[454] And that's why they identify themselves as Jews.

Some are Jews because of their faith. For them, being Jewish is not open to debate: they believe in the God-given Torah and in all the God-given Commandments. They believe, and that's why they are Jews.

Some are Jews out of spite. Their approach to Judaism is echoed in the writings of the philosopher Leo Strauss and in the suggestion made by Emil Fackenheim to establish a new, 614th Commandment: "Jews are forbidden to give Hitler posthumous victories."[455,456] It's a kind of contrarianism where surviving is a moral statement.

And some are Jews because of the values. As they see it, Judaism is a value system they subscribe to. Some even view it as a mission of *tikkun olam,* repairing the world. They are idealists, and that's why they are Jews.

Jewish idealism in its current shape and form is a recent phenomenon facilitated by the Jews' new standing in the world.[457] Because they are no longer singled out as pariahs by the rest of society, at least not officially, and because they have a national political expression in Israel, Jews are somewhat less inclined to look inward anymore and don't have to be totally preoccupied with survival and with preserving and defending their once ostracized community. They have an opportunity to think about things they can do as a group that will benefit the rest of the world. And of course, that is quite ironic: The Jews' social and political normalcy is what enables them to advance a Jewish agenda that is abnormal—an agenda that includes a special mission not expected of other groups.

Rabbi Nachman Krochmal, a prominent scholar of the Jewish Enlightenment movement in Galicia at the beginning of the nineteenth century, addressed this matter at a relatively early stage.[458] His ideas influenced later Jewish thinkers, including Asher Ginsberg (Ahad Ha'am), the poet Hayyim Nahman Bialik, and Rabbi Kook. Krochmal's seminal book, *Guide of the Perplexed of the Time*, which was published posthumously, is not an easy read and conveys a highly ambitious view of the Jewish life cycle.[459] He believed all peoples are subject to inevitable historical processes: birth, growth, and decline. All peoples—except one. The Jewish people are not subject to the "historical laws of decline and demise." Similar to others, he thought, Jews do experience periods of peaks and lows that history brings their way. But unlike others who fade away and disappear after reaching a low point, the Jews recover after each decline, only to reach a new height. Following every low point, the Jews devise new solutions to "the people's needs in our age," which enable them to "preserve their spiritual-cultural identity."[460]

What makes that accomplishment possible? According to Krochmal, who was among the first to envision a modern Jewish mission, the key can be found in the Jewish faith in an all-encompassing God. That faith is what maintains them as a group who refuse to submit to the grinding wheels of time.[461] If the rest of mankind has to take small steps to achieve a better understanding of the existing reality, the Jews are exempt from that journey: The God they believe in is a God that contains all insights. Therefore, their historical role is to "return to the cave" and lead the rest of humanity from there to the recognition of the totality of God's absoluteness.[462]

There's a working assumption here that requires clarification: The Jews have been cast in a special role in the larger human drama, which they must try and fill. It's an important role—whether one calls it "a light unto the nations," as it was commonly designated in the past, or *tikkun olam*, the more popular name today.[463] The essence of the idea is that there's a special people (the Jews) who have a special calling (mission), which will usher in a special time (the Redemption).

Many agreed with that assumption. Even Theodor Herzl, the visionary of the Jewish State, who was never overly drawn to spirituality, wrote in his diary: "For God would not have preserved our people for so long if we did not have another role to play in the history of mankind."[464] Naturally, people didn't always agree on the details of that role, the mission, or how to carry it out. Nor did they agree that the mission itself is a tenet of Jewish theology.[465] The Bible doesn't dictate an explicit message concerning the Jews' mission in the world. As for the universal moral message conveyed in the Books of the Prophets, all sorts of interpretations are possible—some of a broader nature (*tikkun olam* in its universal sense) and some more restrictive (the return of the Jewish people to their land and to God).[466] Either way, one can maintain that for many Jews today the very existence of a calling—regardless of its precise nature—fills the void left by the collapse of the shared belief in a covenant with God. The mission may not be the same one that Krochmal defined (spreading the faith), but it's still the glue that keeps the group together. It's the fuel that supplies the Jews with the justification and strength to persevere in their journey into the future.

Why are the Jews needed? Because they have a role to fulfill. According to the conclusion reached by the (non-Jewish) British historian Paul Johnson, the Jewish people were "appointed to be a pilot project for the entire human race."

And why preserve Judaism? To fulfill that role.

Fragments of thoughts and ideas pertaining to the Jewish role in the world appear in the writings of philosophers from different periods and from diverse schools. Abraham Joshua Heschel preached that "Israel is destined to be a holy people. That is the essence of our mission."[467] Leo Baeck posited that the Jews have a special talent for preserving the idea of a moral monotheism.[468] In his book *Why I am a Jew*, the French author Edmond Fleg romanticized the role of the Jews in laying the foundations for world peace.[469] Rabbi Kook wrote that "our nationality"—the Jews—is meant to "bring general salvation to every person on the face of the earth."[470] The historian Simon Dubnow suggested that "perhaps Jewish history will have a not inconsiderable share in the spiritual change that is to annihilate national intolerance, the modern substitute for the religious bigotry of the Middle Ages."[471] And Martin Buber strove for *tikkun olam* in the spirit of Messianism, on which "the purpose of Judaism in the world rests."[472]

Various insights regarding the essence of the Jewish mission naturally led to different, and often opposite, conclusions about its practical implementation, about what Jews needed to do. Franz Rosenzweig believed that to fulfill their mission as "a sign and miracle," the Jews had to remain dispersed and stateless.[473] Abba Hillel Silver thought just the opposite: it was the existence of a state—Israel—that would make it easier for the Jews in the

Diaspora to achieve their universal mission as a Jewish minority.[474] David Ben-Gurion disagreed with both of them. He believed that the "modern Zionist idea" is actually "the rebirth of the ancient idea of redemption."[475] In other words, the Jews living in Israel, and not the Jews in the Diaspora, will be the ones to fulfill the Jewish mission by establishing an "exemplary state."[476] It's no coincidence that Ben-Gurion was careful to word the opening line of Israel's Proclamation of Independence in a way that alludes to the special role of the people who "gave to the world the eternal Book of Books."[477]

As expected, more recent opinion leaders have tried their hand at the mission garment and still try to do so today. The following is an essentially random sample of them: the American activist and journalist Leonard Fein wrote that "our task is to speak out, to tell what we have seen, to say what we know."[478] According to the Israeli researcher Gidi Grinstein, the Jewish people have "a unique mission in the service of humanity, both in terms of morality and ethics and in finding leadership, resources and practical solutions to global problems."[479] The British rabbi The Lord Jonathan Sacks wrote that Judaism is the "principled defeat of tragedy in the name of hope."[480] Even the American film actor Richard Dreyfuss took a crack at it: "We are a people who stand for a certain thing, a certain sense of justice and freedom."[481]

Special Mission: The Jews, and no other people, were chosen to fill a certain role. And it doesn't matter whether the role was imposed on them by God (which is what the Jews who believe in the God of the Ten Commandments think) or if it's the result of a historical-evolutionary process in which the Jews perfected beliefs and traits that prepare them for repairing the world.[482]

Chosenness: The concept of *tikkun olam*—which articulates an agenda aimed at creating social change—appears in the prayer *Aleinu LeShabeach*, which starts with words of praise for God because "he did not make us like the other nations."[483] The Jews are a distinct group who are required to fill a role they were destined for.

And, as expected, there were Jews who looked askance at the burden of this mission which had been placed on their shoulders. The members of the community who wanted to take advantage of the modern age to normalize the Jewish people were also the ones who realized that normalization meant uprooting that sense of mission. Leon (Yehuda Leib) Pinsker, one of the earliest Zionist thinkers, sought to enable the Jews to "live and be a nation like all the other nations."[484] And the author Yosef Haim Brenner defiantly claimed: "I would, with the most delicious and fierce pleasure, erase from the Hebrew prayer book of our generation any mention of 'You have chosen us from among the nations.'"[485] In his book *Between Right and Right*, the Israeli author A. B. Yehoshua contended that the solution to the problem of the Jews is "not in changing the world and adapting it to the special nature of our existence, but rather in changing the nature of Jewish existence and adapting it to the world."[486]

So, as we see, distinctiveness and having a mission can often meet objections. Because these factors underscore Jewish tribalism, they separate Jews from the rest of the world, which they want to be part of. They also set a high standard for the Jews, and it's not altogether clear that the Jews can or want to meet it.[487] That standard has often been exploited by the Jews' enemies when trying to prove that Jews are not as good as they claim or are supposed to be. Lastly, they reinforce the view that the Jews, as a people, have been endowed with a surplus of virtues. Many Jews consider that kind of idea as racist. And what Jew wants to be accused of racism—the most despicable of all the ideologies that led to their own persecution?

And it's worth noting that the message of a universal calling is stressed more frequently by liberal Jewish thinkers in the Diaspora than it is by Jewish conservatives in Israel.[488] It's an interesting paradox that also has a clear political context. It's the theorists and spokesmen of the politically conservative (and religiously Orthodox) Jewish school of thought who have no particular problem with the Jews as chosen people, a treasured nation—and yet they're the ones who display a natural distrust for the demand that the chosen people make a special contribution to the rest of the world.[489] On the other hand, it's the theorists and spokesmen of the liberal (and religiously Progressive) Jewish school of thought who are highly uncomfortable with the idea of "chosenness" and often maintain that it's unseemly or even conveys a trace of tribal arrogance—although they are the most vocal in their demand that Jews fill their cart with an item containing universal *tikkun olam*.[490]

There are Jews by virtue of emotion, and Jews by virtue of reason. There are Jews who investigate questions of identity and Jews whose identity is effortless, natural, and uncomplicated.

And there are Jews who make do with faith—and those who also need a mission.

All of them are challenged by the vibrant world of the twenty-first century—a world after Spinoza and Nietzsche, Copernicus and Darwin, where it's more challenging to defend faith.[491] We are living in a global world that undermines tribal and political boundaries, a multicultural world that makes assimilation easy, and a technological world that appears to have the ability to erode the power of historical memory.

In such a world, the question of why be Jewish is a critical one. It's a question that has no simple answer. Who needs all the effort? Who needs the investment and the organization, the persistence and the struggle, the blood and the money, the reflection and the debate? Why should anyone care if there are Jews, and why is it good for the Jews to be Jews in the first place?

It's a question that every individual Jew must ask himself and answer, and about which Jewish leadership owes an answer to the community. In our day and age, Jews need to address that question more than ever because, unlike in the past, the Judaism that many of them practice no longer rests on any accepted religious belief or distinct social milieu. Every Jew today might feel that he or she has a reasonable alternative that does not entail a forced or humiliating transition to another group with which they can affiliate. And unlike the past, there's no social price for leaving. So maybe there's no special reason to stay. In a world where the Jews comprise barely one-fifth of 1 percent of the global population, maybe the natural default is to gradually disappear.

So why remain? We've already answered that question: life's reality, personal ties, faith, spite, and, of course, a sense of mission and calling.

And here's another possible answer: why not?

The philosopher Leo Strauss provided a contrarian and provocative answer when he wrote the following: "The disgraceful character of the only alternative" available to the undecided Jew is "denying one's origin, past or heritage."[492] But it's possible, and even desirable, to take the edge off his answer by offering a different option with a more positive tone.

Tragedies, wars, venomous speech, and persistent and hateful enemies all make it easy to forget that the present situation of Jews is still much better than it was throughout most of Jewish history. The present situation also facilitates a more diverse and animated internal Jewish space: You can be a Jew today in multiple shapes and forms, belong to several different denominations, express a broad range of opinions, and highlight preferred themes. You can be religious or secular, Reform or Orthodox, Sephardic or Ashkenazi, Israeli or French, a member of a synagogue, or a Federation supporter (or belong to nothing). You can believe in God, or not. You can be a Zionist or an anti-Zionist. You can be a liberal or a conservative. You can insist on repairing the world or insist on fulfilling the 613 Commandments.

Why be Jewish? Because a Jewish life is a spacious place with an abundance of options. A Jewish life is the most ancient kind in the world and continues to revitalize itself each and every day.

Why be Jewish? Because the Jewish life is a multifaceted and exciting world. And as long as you remain within its boundaries, as blurry as they may be, a Jewish life creates a framework of identity and commitment, fosters a feeling of pride and satisfaction, challenges one's thinking and daily endeavors, provides meaning, and preserves a sense of belonging and continuity.

In short, everything a Jew needs.

Endnotes

1 Joseph Dan, "Jewish History in the Post-Narrative Age," in Joseph Dan, *Chaos Theory and the Study of History*, Dvir, 2009, 169 [Hebrew]. Dan articulates the Jewish people's difficulty to continue existing without the ability to tell a greater historical story. The "Jewish people" is, of course, a later depiction. The earlier ones are the "people of Israel," the "Hebrews," the "Israelites," etc.

2 The British historian Paul Johnson underscored the Jews' documentation capacity. See Paul Johnson, *A History of the Jews*, Harper & Row, 1987, 7. Johnson writes: "The Jews are the only people in the world today who possess a historical record, however obscure in places, which allows them to trace their origins back into very remote times."

3 Jacob Katz attributed "the unity of the Jewish people" in different places and different periods to a "common faith, national tradition, and hope for future redemption." See: Jacob Katz, *Tradition and Crisis: Jewish Society at the End of the Middle Ages*, Bialik Institute, 1957, 15 [Hebrew].

4 For more about Abraham's revolution, see: Jon D. Levenson, Inheriting Abraham: The Legacy of the Patriarch in Judaism, Christianity, and Islam, Princeton University Press, 2012; and David Klinghoffer, The Discovery of God: Abraham and the Birth of Monotheism, Doubleday, 2003. For more about Moses, see: Micah Goodman, Moses's Final Speech, Dvir, 2014 [Hebrew].

5 The transition from "Hebrews" to "Jews" who are focused on the written text is attributed to the days of Ezra. See: Michael L. Satlow, *Creating Judaism*, Columbia University Press, 1996. The Talmud attributes the start of the learning revolution to Hillel the Elder (the end of the first century BCE). The major competitor to studying Torah—the sacrificial rites—no longer played a role in Jewish life following the destruction of the Temple. See also: Gedalyahu Alon, *Jews, Judaism, and the Classical World: Studies in Jewish History in the Times of the Second Temple and Talmud.* trans. Israel Abrahams, Magnes Press, 1977.

6 We have no conclusive evidence about who actually codified the Mishnah and the Talmud and why they did so. For a popular and simple explanation of the subject, see: Harry Freedman, *The Talmud: A Biography*, Bloomsbury, 2014.

7 This distinction appears in different versions in multiple sources, but is articulated in simple terms by Arthur Hertzberg and Aron Hirt-Manheimer in *Jews: The Essence and Character of a People*, HarperCollins, 1998.

8 There is, of course, an understandable inclination to highlight the turmoil, changes and crises. But it's worth noting that the Jews also enjoyed long periods of (relative) serenity and (relative) well-being in many places. The Jews in Babylonia are the most striking example.

9 For more about the theory that it's not Judaism which undergoes crises, but rather only the "Jews" who experience them, see: Yeshayahu Leibowitz, *Faith, History and Values,* Academon, 2002 [Hebrew]. Leibowitz writes: "There are no times of crisis in Judaism. The Jewish people face periods of crisis, just like all other peoples and societies face periods of crisis, and there are periods of crisis in the life of an individual as an individual, crises that are associated with his biological reality and his social reality. But in Judaism, as a system of faith and of observance of the Torah and the Commandments, there is no crisis because the very essence of the religious experience is man's crisis."

10 Including the Babylonian-Iraqi community that existed uninterruptedly for over two thousand years.

11 The Hasmonean Kingdom was the "only period of complete political emancipation in the annals of the people and the land, from the days of the First Temple and up to the establishment of the State of Israel." See: Uriel Rappaport, "The Hasmonean State (160–37 BCE)," in *The History of the Land of Israel—The Hellenist Period and the Hasmonean State*, ed. Menachem Stern. Ben Zvi Institute, Keter, 1981 [Hebrew].

12 David Novak suggested a somewhat different version of the condition of the modern Jew: "Modernity has been largely shaped for Jews by three momentous experiences: the acquisition of citizenship by individual Jews in secular nation-states, the destruction of one-third of Jewry in the Holocaust, and the founding of the State of Israel." See: the beginning of the first chapter in David Novak, *Natural Law in Judaism*, Cambridge University Press, 2008. For more about when and under what circumstances the current period in Jewish history exactly began, see: Michael A. Meyer, "Where Does the Modern Period of Jewish History Begin?" in *Judaism: A Quarterly Journal of Jewish Life and Thought* 24 (Summer 1975): 329–38. The article compares the different opinions of historians who regard certain political circumstances as the beginning of the modern period in Jewish history (according to Shmuel Ettinger, the key to the change in the Jews' condition can be attributed to the emergence of the centralized absolutistic states) with those who prefer to assign it to philosophical developments (Heinrich Graetz believed that Moses Mendelssohn signaled the advent of the new age) and with those who underscore social changes (Salo Baron focuses on migrations, capitalism and other aspects of social change).

13 The crisis that Judaism is facing today actually started much earlier: It began with the dismantling of Jewish communal institutions in the Diaspora, the Enlightenment and the Emancipation. All those processes compelled the Jews to adapt to a new reality in which the strength of the community (in the

Diaspora) weakened, the power of religion diminished (for most Jews), and the relationship with the non-Jewish world (in the Diaspora and later in Israel as well) underwent a profound and dramatic change.

14 S. M. Dubnow, *Jewish History: An Essay in the Philosophy of History*, n.d., n.p., 177. The complete quote better clarifies Dubnow's intent: "Jewry, being a spiritual entity, cannot suffer annihilation: the body, the mold, may be destroyed, the spirit is immortal." I wish to add that when researching the book, I read an English translation of Dubnow's writings and not the original version. The same holds true for other works written in languages I'm not in proficient in (German, Russian, French, etc.), whose English or Hebrew translation I read and quoted from. Dubnow was murdered in Riga in 1941.

15 For further reading, see: Meyer Waxman, "R. Joseph Albo's Approach to the Principles of Religion and Its Relationship to the Thought of His Contemporaries, R. Hasdai Crescas and R. Simeon ben Tzemach Duran," Yavne, 1956, 153–156 [Hebrew].

16 Joseph Albo was one of the most important rabbis in Spain in the fourteenth and fifteenth centuries. The source of the quote is *Sefer HaIkarim*, article 1, chapter 4 [Hebrew].

17 See: Moshe Gresser, *Dual Allegiance: Freud as a Modern Jew*, SUNY Press, 1994, 242. The subsequent Freud quotes are from Avshalom Elitzur, "Liberators of the Mind: Jews and Judaism Within the Psychoanalytic Movement," in *New Jewish Time: Jewish Culture in a Secular Age*, ed. Yirmiyahu Yovel, Keter, 2007 [Hebrew], and from Sigmund Freud, *Totem and Taboo,* trans. Ruth Ginsburg, Resling, 2013 (a newer and more current Hebrew translation).

18 Based on the preface he wrote to *Totem and Taboo* and other writings, Freud didn't have any special affinity with the Jewish religion nor did he identify with Jewish nationalism, which began taking root at the time. The Land of Israel has never produced anything "apart from holy religious madness," Freud wrote in a letter to Arnold Zweig in 1932, which was quoted in Yerushalmi (see the following endnote). At the initiative of the translator, the Hebrew translation of *Totem and Taboo* contains several references to Judaism which did not appear in the original (Freud was ambivalent about that initiative). See: Eran Rolnik, *Freud in Zion: History of Psychoanalysis in Jewish Palestine/Israel* 1918–1948, Am Oved, 2007. [Hebrew].

19 Sigmund Freud, *Moses and Monotheism*, Martino Fine Books, 2010. This is a reprint of the original 1939 edition. For a better understanding of the theory put forward in the book and its connection with Freud's biography and the spectrum of his views, see: Yosef Hayim Yerushalmi, *Freud's Moses*, Yale University Press, 1991. Freud suggests that Judaism may have reached "moral heights that remained unobtainable by other peoples in the ancient world."

20 Whether the Jews were really the first to embrace a monotheistic religion has been an ongoing topic of debate. (Many researchers, including those who wrote

in response to *Moses and Monotheism*, consider Pharaoh Akhenaten to be the first monotheist. See, for example, Israel Knohl, *Where Did We Come From: The Bible's Genetic Code*, Dvir, 2008 [Hebrew]. Professor Yehuda Elitzur suggested that it was biblical Joseph who turned Akhenaten into a monotheist. Some researchers have said that Akhenaten and Moses are the same person). Another popular view posited by researchers of ancient history is that the Israelite religion in biblical times was not monotheistic. The Hebrews believed that they had to worship only one god, but did not rule out the existence of other gods. For a brief explanation about monotheism and its sources, it's worth reading William Wainwright, "Monotheism," in *The Stanford Encyclopedia of Philosophy*, ed. Edward N. Zalta, 2013, fall edition. http://plato.stanford.edu/archieves/fall2013/entries/monotheism

21 See: Yehezkel Kaufmann, *A History of the Religion of Israel, vol. 2*, Bialik Institute, Dvir, 1953, 225 ff. [Hebrew]. With regard to Jewish continuity, Kaufmann believed that "when former lifestyles and beliefs are no longer valid, the continuity of the people has to be shifted from the milieu to literature, from the emotional and subconscious sphere to the conscious intellectual sphere. Classical literature is needed in these cases in order to define Jewish identity and create a commitment to it." For more about the subject, see: David Shachar, "The Historical-Cultural Heritage and its Educational Significance in Yehezkel Kaufmann's Theory," *Maof ve'Maase* 5 (1999) [Hebrew]. For a clear and concise analysis of the relationship between Judaism and idolatry and its present implications, it is highly recommended to read Asa Kasher, *Judaism and Paganism*, Israel Ministry of Defense. The University on the Air, 2004 [Hebrew].

22 For more about the expectations that Jews in the Diaspora and Israel have of this partnership, see: Shmuel Rosner and Avi Gil, *Jewish and Democratic: Perspectives from World Jewry,* The Jewish People Policy Institute, 2014.

23 Guttmann's seminal work, which he completed when the Nazis rose to power and right before he fled Germany and came to Israel, is called *The Philosophy of Judaism.* It was published in Hebrew under the same name by the Bialik Institute in 1952. It was translated by Y. L. Baruch.

24 Secularization processes rest on the development of science and research, but also on the emergence of ideological movements such as nationalism (Jewish and others) and socialism (which many members of the Jewish elite flocked to).

25 The Guttmann quotes are taken from "About the Foundations of Judaism," in *Religion and Science*, Magnes Press, 1979, 259 [Hebrew].

26 See also: Moshe Halbertal, "Between Jewish Studies and Jewish Religion," in *Jewish Thought and Jewish Belief*, ed. Daniel J. Lasker, The BGI Press, 2012 [Hebrew]. Halbertal describes the shakeup that Judaism experienced when the two elements "on which the believer's foundation and authority rest" were undermined—the idea of revelation and the idea of tradition—and he too quotes Guttmann.

27 The book, written in Arabic in the ninth century, was translated into Hebrew in the eleventh century (we don't know by whom). Two later translations were provided by Rabbi Judah ibn Tibbon, and in the twentieth century by Rabbi Yosef Kapach. The quote that appears here is from the Kapach edition of *The Book of Beliefs and Opinions*, 132 [Hebrew].

28 Guttmann himself, as well as other researchers who studied rabbinic literature, such as Efraim Elimelech Urbach (see: *The Sages—Their Concepts and Beliefs*, 4 [Hebrew]), maintain that the Talmud never defined clear "principles" of Jewish faith. "However, it definitely allowed us to establish a common fundamental format of faith," Guttmann wrote in "The Religious Ideas of Talmudic Judaism," in *Philosophies of Judaism*, Holt, Rinehart and Winston, 1964, 34 ff. Rasag's use of the plural form of "teachings" was against the Karaites (who recognized only the written Torah).

29 Over the years, a number of interpretations of what Rasag wrote were proposed, which take some of the sting out of that literal reading. See, for example, the essay written by Rabbi Yehuda Amital, "About the Status and Treatment of the Secular Jew Today." [Hebrew]. Amital writes: "That statement has quite a different meaning than the one usually assigned to it. It is generally understood as saying that the Jews are a people only if we strictly observe the Torah and its Commandments. And failure to do so, heaven forbid, means the end of Jewish peoplehood. But that is not what Rasag had in mind at all. A Jew remains a Jew and the Jewish people remain the Jewish people even when they fail to observe the Torah." According to Amital, the intention behind Rasag's statement was to declare the victory of the Torah."

30 Refer to the previous endnote in the matter of the principles of faith according to the Talmud. It's worth adding that the Talmud itself contains a number of attempts to define the entire Torah "on one leg"—the two most famous ones are by Rabbi Akiva ("love your neighbor as yourself") and by Hillel ("what is hateful to you, do not do to others"). Their attempts, however, fall short of a systematic presentation of the principles of Judaism.

31 It appears in his commentary on the Book of Exodus. See *The Commentaries of Rabbi Saadia Gaon on the Torah*, Mossad Harav Kook, 1963, 175–176 [Hebrew]. See also: Haggai Ben Shammai, "The Ten Principles of Faith of Rabbi Saadia Gaon" in *Daat* 37, 26–11 [Hebrew]. It's worth nothing that Philo of Alexandria, who lived in an earlier period, wrote about the principles of faith that emerge, among other things, from the grouping of laws under the Ten Commandments.

32 Throughout the generations, a number of prominent attempts were made to draft "principles" of Judaism, which are characterized by fundamental and stylistic differences. Rabbi Joseph Albo (from the fourteenth and fifteenth centuries), who examined the principles defined by Maimonides, reduced them to three: the existence of God, the divine origin of the Torah, and providence through reward and punishment.

33 The Mishnah's commentary on Maimonides, Tractate Sanhedrin, chapter 10.

34 Amos Oz and Fania Oz-Salzberger, *Jews and Words*, Keter, 2014. The authors write, "Had we told the prophet Amos that he was Jewish, he would have agreed with us: He is indeed a member of the Tribe of Judah and a native of the city of Tekoa. But had we told him he belonged to the 'Jewish people,' that terminology would have meant nothing to him…in all the generations prior to the nineteenth century, the Jews called themselves 'the children of Israel' or 'the people of Israel.'" The first use of the term "Judaism" appears in 2 Maccabees, which was written around the year 124 BCE. See: Michael I. Satlow, "Defining Religion: Accounting for 'Religions' in the Study of Religion," in *Journal of the American Academy of Religion*, 74 (2006). In the same context, it's interesting to read what Professor Noam Pianko has to say about the renewed use of the term "Jewish people." Pianko talks about the currently popular notion of "peoplehood" and maintains that it too was engendered by the need to address present day challenges of identity, while wearing away at the Jews' earlier commonalities and resulting in a tautological definition: What unifies the Jews is the fact that they're unified. See: Noam Pianko, *Jewish Peoplehood: An American Innovation*, Rutgers University Press, 2015.

35 Emmanuel Levinas, *Difficult Freedom: Essays on Judaism*. trans. Sean Hand. Johns Hopkins University Press, 1990, 24.

36 Daniel Boyarin says that Christianity is what invented Judaism. "One cannot speak of Judaism as existing before Christianity." See: Daniel Boyarin, *Border Lines: The Partition of Judaeo-Christianity*, University of Pennsylvania Press, 2004, 11. The French philosopher Jean-Paul Sartre claimed that Jews became Jews by the antisemites. If there's a connection between the two, "it's because they live in a community that regards them as Jews." The full text of George J. Becker's English translation of Sartre's book, *Anti-Semite and Jew* (1944), is available online: http://abahlali.org/files/Jean-Paul_Sartre_Anti-Semite_and_Jew_An Exploration_of_the_Etiology_of_Hate_1995.pdf.

37 Marx was the son of a Jew who converted to Christianity. His major essay on the subject, *On the Jewish Question*, was written in 1843. The quote here is taken from David Nuremberg, *Anti-Judaism: The Western Tradition*, W.W. Norton, 2013.

38 One of Toynbee's biographers admitted that "while it is wrong to call him anti-Semitic, it remains true that Toynbee was profoundly unsympathetic to Judaism and to Jews." See: William H. McNeil, *Arnold J. Toynbee: A Life*, Oxford University Press, 1989. The best known event that links Professor Toynbee with Jewish history and Israel is his confrontation with Yaacov Herzog, who served as Israel's ambassador to Canada. For a relatively new description of that confrontation, see: Yair Rosenberg, "When an Israeli Ambassador Debated a British Historian on Israel's Legitimacy—and Won," in *Tablet Magazine*, January 31, 2014. The first part of the debate is available online. "The Herzog-Toynbee

Debate Part 1/8: Israel: Morality and History." Forever Blue and White. YouTube, February 9, 2011. Video, 10:25. (Transcript available). https://www.youtube.com/watch?v=2M5Ntu3C0IA. An interesting reply to Toynbee's claims was also written by the historian Jacob Talmon. See: *Unity and Uniqueness—Essays in Historical Thought*. Schocken, 1965, 229 [Hebrew]. Talmon wrote his ideas in an article dealing with the "universal and unique significance" of Judaism as a response to Professor Toynbee's attacks. Shalom Salomon Wald writes that Toynbee later changed his views on the Jewish question in his book *Rise and Decline of Civilizations: Lessons for the Jewish People*, Academic Studies Press, 2014.

39 Timothy Synder, Black Earth: The Holocaust as History and Warning, The Bodley Head, 2015.

40 Scholem's quote is taken from Rachel Elior, *What Kind of Religion is Judaism? part I,* Odyssey, 2015 [Hebrew].

41 Philipp Bloch,"Biographie des Dr. H. Graetz," in Michael Brenner, *Prophets of the Past: Interpreters of Jewish History*, trans. Steven Rendall, Princeton University Press, 2010.

42 Nahum Norbert Glatzer, *The Judaic Tradition: Texts*, Behrman House, 1982, 514. For more about Yom Tov Lippmann (Leopold) Zunz, see: Nahum Glatzer, *Yom Tov Lippmann Zunz: The Man, His Life and Creation (1794–1886)*, Magnes Press, 1988 [Hebrew].

43 The meeting was held in the home of Rabbi Michael Sachs (1808–1864), who collaborated with Zunz on writing a new translation of the Bible.

44 Michael A. Meyer, *Ideas of Jewish History*, Behrman House, 1974, 218.

45 See: Heinrich Graetz, *The Construction of Jewish History*. Originally published in 1846.

46 The Jews didn't always make an effort to keep historical records. For many years, they couldn't be bothered to write a history for themselves. The Second Temple was destroyed in the first century AD, and its destruction was documented by the historian Flavius Josephus. Following that, for a period of 1,500 years, the writers of the times kept silent. That was the case until 1573, when an Italian Jew by the name of Bonito de' Rossi—who is better known as Azariah min HaAdumim—wrote his book *Me'or Enayim*. The book led to a heated debate because he dared to question, even a little, the historical authenticity of some of the legends of the Sages. The Jewish American historian Yosef Haim Yerushalmi talked about this long absence of works on Jewish history. See: Yosef Haim Yerushalmi, *Zakhor: Jewish History and Jewish Memory*, University of Washington Press, 1982. For more about de' Rossi and the controversy over his book, see the introduction by the translator of the book's English version: *Azariah de' Rossi*, trans. Joanna Weinberg, Yale University Press, 2001. See also: Avner Falk, *A Psychoanalytic History of the Jews*, Associated University Presses,

1996, 341. De' Rossi's book was banned by Italy's rabbis and he died a few years after it was published.

47 In one of his books, Baron complained that the history of American Jewry has a hard time finding its place in the overall Jewish narrative because "it was unable to present an unbroken chain of pogroms and edicts." See: Salo Baron, *The Test of Liberty*: *Chapters in the History of American Jews*, Schocken, 1977, 5 [Hebrew].

48 Michael Brenner, *Prophets of the Past*: *Interpreters of Jewish History,* trans. Stephen Randall. Princeton University Press, 2010.

49 Haim Hillel Ben-Sasson's introduction to Avraham Malamat, et al. *The History of the Jewish People in Ancient Times*, 21 [Hebrew]. Ben-Sasson's argument is not as pointed or extreme as its tone may suggest. To pay it justice, here's the sentence in its entirety: "Know that a kind of 'national identity' comprised of assimilated, and even converted, Jews has emerged. In contrast to them, there is a tide of modern national Jewish nationalism, which is aware of the challenges of the new period and has reached the height of its achievements in creating the State of Israel."

50 Ben-Sasson, 18.

51 The limited scope of this book necessitates making generalizations that are insensitive to the nuances in the different historians' interpretations of the essence of Jewish existence. For example, Yosef Gorny noted that "according to Jost and Graetz, the Jews are a spiritual nation; Dubnow and Baron believed that Jews are a society that has a national and religious, and primarily diasporic, foundation; Dinur and Mahler were of the opinion that Jews are a nationality with a connection to their national territory—the Land of Israel; and Ettinger was somewhere in between the last two views." See: Yosef Gorny, "Klal Israel from Halakha to History, in *Contemporary Jewries*: *Convergence and Divergence,* ed. Eliezer Ben-Rafael, et al. Brill, 2003, and Reuven Michael, " Jost, Graetz and Dubnow on the Singularity of Jewish History," in *Transformation and Changes in Modern Jewish History*: *Essays Presented in Honor of Shmuel Ettinger*, ed. Shmuel Almog, et al. Zalman Shazar Center, 1988 [Hebrew].

52 The Babylonian Talmud's Tractate Suta contains a lengthy discussion about how many covenants God entered into with the Jewish people. See Suta 37 and the wealth of commentaries on the subject. See also: Israel Knohl, *A King of Flesh and Blood*. Shalom Hartman Institute [Hebrew]. Knohl describes the singularity of the biblical covenant compared to covenants of other ancient peoples. Max Weber also dealt at length with the idea of the covenant. See: Max Weber, *Ancient Judaism*, trans. Hans H. Gerth and Don Martindale, Free Press, 1952. For more about Weber's perspective on the biblical covenant, see: Ernest W. Nicholson, *God and His People*: *Covenant and Theology in the Old Testament*, Clarendon, 1986, 38.

53 Daniel Elazar focused on the idea of the covenant in *Covenant as the Basis of the Jewish Political Tradition* and in greater detail in the book he co-authored: Daniel Elazar and Stuart Cohen, *The Jewish Polity: Jewish Political Organization from Biblical Times to the Present*, Indiana University Press, 1984. The authors write that "Jewish tradition is initially concerned with relationships and not structures." David Hartman also underscored the idea of the covenant as a pillar of Jewish tradition. See: David Hartman, *A Living Covenant: The Innovative Spirit in Traditional Judaism*, Jewish Lights Publishing, 1997 (originally published in 1985). Hartman writes: "The concepts of divine self-limitation and human freedom and responsibility are reflected in the description of the Creation in Genesis and in the covenants of Noah, Abraham, and Sinai." Hartman distinguishes five covenant phases: Creation, Noah, Abraham, Sinai, and Oral Law. The Talmud provides an interesting answer to the question about when the covenant was signed, assigning the significant time to the days of the Book of Esther. See: Babylonian Talmud *Shabbat* 88. Also refer to the engaging discussion of this issue in Emmanuel Levinas, *Nine Talmudic Readings*, trans. Annette Aronowicz, Indiana University Press, 1990. It's worth noting that a Reform interpretation of the idea of the covenant was inclined to strip it of its national substance and limit it to a description of the relationship between man and God, thereby bringing the Jewish concept closer to that of comparable religions. Furthermore, it's interesting to mention Joshua Berman's perspective, who views the covenant not only as a collective matter, but also as "the delegation of authority to each individual." In other words, God has a covenant "with every individual who belongs to that collective." See: Joshua Berman, "Every Individual is a King," *Tchelet*, 2007 [Hebrew].

54 Hertzberg and Hirt-Manheimer, 15. Hertzberg was a highly influential American Jewish author and historian.

55 Elazar actually relates the communal organization model that existed among the ancient Tribes of Israel and up to the establishment of the Jewish Federations of America, and even the way pre-State Israel organized itself, to the "covenant" tradition.

56 Rabbi Soloveitchik (1903–1993), one of the most prominent leaders of American Jewry in recent generations, was born in Belarus and emigrated to the United States at the beginning of the 1930s. He belonged to the ultra-Orthodox Agudath Israel, but following the Holocaust and the establishment of the State of Israel, he joined the Zionist-religious Mizrahi movement. The quote here is from *Kol Dodi Dofek: Listen–My Beloved Knocks*, trans. David Z. Gordon, Ktav Publishing House, 2000. Soloveitchik writes: "To begin with, the Israelites in Egypt were a camp; when God freed them, they attained the rank of a people." Many commentaries have been written about Soloveitchik's concept of the covenant, and what is presented here naturally doesn't exhaust the discussion. For more about the sources of Soloveitchik's concept of the covenant and an

understanding of the impact of other thinkers (Barth, Brunner) on his theory, see Alan Brill, "A Victory Without a Battle: A Dialectic Approach to Rabbi Soloveitchik's Philosophy," in *A Rabbi in a New Word,* ed. Avinoam Rosenak and Naftali Rothenberg, Van Leer Institute and Magnes Press, 2010 [Hebrew].

57 In the original: "The national development is based upon an all-pervasive religious tradition, which lives in the soul of the people as the Sinaitic Revelation, the Law of Moses...not a simple political or racial entity, but, to an eminent degree, a spiritual people." See: Dubnow, 13–14.

58 Questions pertaining to the essence of the Redemption have been discussed by many different thinkers, including Shalom, Levinas, and Kook. Also, Franz Rosenzweig, a modern Jewish thinker, believed that the Redemption is one of the three principles that the essence of Judaism rests on—"creation, revelation, redemption." For a brief discussion of the use Rosenzweig made of those notions, see: David Ellenson, "Eternity and Time," in *20th Century Jewish Religious Thought*, ed. Arthur A. Cohen and Paul Mendes-Flohr, Jewish Publication Society, 2010, 189. A brief yet exhaustive description of the different concepts of redemption prior to the modern age can also be found in the article "Exile and Redemption in Judaism's Mystery," by Israel Weinstock in *Redemption and State—The Redemption of Israel, Vision and Reality*: *People and State According to Judaism,* Israel Ministry of Education, Religious Culture Department, 1979 [Hebrew].

59 Some of the more prominent authors of Hebrew literature in the early days of Zionism, such as Brenner, Smolenskin and Berdichevsky, believed there was no way to present Judaism as a "school of philosophy with its own distinctive substance." See: "Jewish People, Jewish Philosophy—Spiritual School or Historical Existence," in Menachem Brinker, *The Modernization and Secularization of Jewish Thought, n.d., n.p.* [Hebrew].

60 This view was articulated quite bluntly in Israel by Yeshayahu Leibowitz. See: Yeshayahu Leibowitz, *Judaism, the People of Israel and the State of Israel*, Schocken, 2005 [Hebrew]. As he saw it: "Judaism does not exist unless it imposes a regime and a certain way of life on a person that affects everyday matters." (The quote is from a Jewish Studies seminar held in Haifa in 1953. See: the Leibowitz website: http://www.leibowitz.co.il/leibarticles.asp?id=31. Heschel was highly critical of that view, which he called "religious behaviorism" and denounced it as "a spiritual wasteland, in the absence of the soul" (see: Dror Bondi, ed., *God Believes in Man*: *Abraham Joshua Heschel's Judaism, Zionism and Social Justice*, The Schechter Institute of Jewish Studies, 2011 [Hebrew].

61 Kaplan, one of the most distinguished leaders of American Jewry in recent generations, founded the Reconstructionist movement. He was born in Vilna in 1881 and died in the United States in 1983. The quote is taken from the electronic edition of his book *Judaism as a Civilization*: *Toward a Reconstruction of American-Jewish Life*, 535.

62 The Kingdom of David and Solomon, if it ever existed, dates back to the eleventh and tenth centuries BCE. Archaeologists continue to debate the scope and nature of the kingdom, and every new finding produces a host of polemics dealing with the period—which is not devoid of ideological or political connotations.

63 Satlow puts it this way: "To be a Jew is to make, primarily, a historical claim… It is to identify with a narrative…that extends back to Abraham…and that is linked to God's covenant." See: Michael L. Satlow, *Creating Judaism*, Columbia University Press, 2006, 10. Jacob Neusner says that Judaism has three components: a worldview, a way of life, and a particular social group. See: Jacob Neusner, *Introduction to American Judaism: What Books Say, What the People Do*, Wipf and Stock, 1994, 31.

64 At present, those Jews are a minority in Israel, and it appears that their strength has been compromised by demographic and cultural trends that are fortifying the camp that wants to maintain the country's unmistakable "Jewish" character. Jews in other parts of the world also want Israel to maintain its Jewish character, although the meaning of Jewish character is the subject of a fiery debate between different groups. See: Shmuel Rosner and Gil, *Jewish and Democratic: Perspectives from World Jewry*.

65 Most researchers of Jewish Orthodoxy agree with Jacob Katz and believe that it's a relatively recent invention which contains many new elements that were formulated in response to the challenges of modern life. See, for example: Moshe Samet, *Chapters in the History of Orthodoxy*, Carmel, 2005 [Hebrew]. See also: Michael Silber, "The Emergence of Ultra-Orthodoxy: The Invention of a Tradition," in *The Uses of Tradition: Jewish Continuity in the Modern Era*, ed. Jack Wertheimer, Jewish Theological Seminary of America, 1992. But there are some researchers who believe that theory which posits that Orthodoxy is a totally modern invention is overstating the matter. For more about that opposing view, see: Benjamin Brown, "The Da'at Torah Doctrine: Three Stages," in *The Path of the Spirit: The Eliezer Schweid Jubilee—Volume II*. ed. Yehoyada Amir. Van Leer Institute, 2005 [Hebrew]. It's worth noting that Orthodoxy is primarily a reaction of European Judaism to changes occurring in the world. Sephardic Jewish sages reacted to "changes in the modern age in a creative and interesting manner, without adopting the same European approach or any European Jewish approach." See: Zvi Zohar, *The Luminous Face of the East*, Hakibbutz Hameuchad, 2001 [Hebrew].

66 This is obviously a highly simplistic representation of a complex concept, which led to heated debates within the Reform movement in different periods. For an engaging description of the various aspects of the Reform approach, see: Michael A. Meyer, *Response to Modernity: A History of the Reform Movement in Judaism*, Oxford University Press, 1988. For more about the Pittsburgh Platform, which, more than anything any other document, symbolized the

attempt to erase the national element from Judaism (but was never adopted as an official position of the entire movement), see: Walter Jacob, ed. *The Changing World of Reform Judaism: The Pittsburgh Platform in Retrospect*, Rodef Shalom Congregation, 1985.

67 The author, Peretz Smolenskin, was apparently the first to declare that there is no necessary connection between fulfilling the Commandments and belonging to the Jewish people. As he wrote in his essay "It is Time to Plant," written between 1875–1878, [Hebrew]: "Because everyone born a Jew shall declare: I am a son of this people, and as long as that feeling exists, the brotherhood will not be breached nor will the power of the entire people, and it will not be diminished from generation to generation, because even those who may abandon some or many of our religious practices will nonetheless keep a share in the inheritance of Israel, as long as their sins are against religion and not against their people." For more about Smolenskin and his views about the Jewish people, see also: Hillel Halkin, "The Novelist of Jewish Unity," *Mosaic*, 2015. The way that Zionist leaders treated the Jewish religion and its contribution to human civilization is at times reminiscent of antisemitic propaganda. For more about that subject see: Joachim Doron, "Classic Zionism and Modern Anti-Semitism: Parallels and Influences (1883–1914)," *Studies in Zionism* 3 (1983). The Jewish Enlightenment and its philosophical origins, coupled with the socialist leanings of many Zionist thinkers, intensified Zionism's fundamental disdain for religion in general and for the Jewish religion, in particular. As explained in a previous note, Noam Pianko's research teaches us that the notion of "peoplehood" assumed a similar role in American Judaism, where it wore away at religious identity and underscored national identity. Pianko stresses the contribution made by Mordecai Kaplan and Stephen Wise to that process.

68 See: Moshe Idel, "The Rise and Decline of the Historical Jew," in *The Past and Beyond It,* ed. Amir Horowitz, et al. The Open University of Israel, 2006, 174 [Hebrew].

69 Mordecai Kaplan, "On the Reconstruction of the Conception of Jewish Nationhood," in *Iyunim Bitkumat Israel*, 13 (2003): 97–113 [Hebrew]. Most of Kaplan's ideas appear in his seminal work, *Judaism as a Civilization: Toward a Reconstruction of American Jewish Life*, 1934.

70 Kaplan's theory is too all-encompassing to describe here. He didn't believe that Jews needed justification for wanting to sustain their culture because he viewed it as a natural aspiration. Nonetheless, he felt that the prospects of that natural desire to prevail and exist in the future would be significantly improved if it had an ethical foundation.

71 Kaplan is not the only thinker who proposed a format for the Jewish religion that isn't dependent on the belief in a supernatural god. Many other attempts are also worthy of study and enrich the Jewish philosophy bookshelf with fascinating ideas. See, for example, Ron Margolin's book, *Inner Religion*, Bar-

Ilan University Press and the Shalom Hartman Institute, 2011 [Hebrew]. Margolin suggests that the Jews' subjective search for God itself embodies religious meaning (even if they don't find God). Margolin's ideas are consistent with those of other thinkers, such as Hans Jonas, who refuse to view religious subjectivity as a weakness in the validity of the religious argument. In his book *Prayer After "the Death of God": A Phenomenological Study in Hebrew Literature*, Bar-Ilan University Press, 2011 [Hebrew], Avi Sagi suggests that prayer is not contingent on the belief in God. I wish to note that both of the above books (as well as Kaplan's highly influential writings) offer a bold, novel and exciting worldview. However, they do not address the practical aspects of the feasibility of Jewish existence that derive from their ideas. And simply put, they don't provide an answer to the question (and perhaps they're unable to do so) about whether the format they propose has sufficient force to guarantee a Jewish legacy that can be passed down to the next generations.

72 For the similarities and differences between Ahad Ha'am and Kaplan, who in many ways was his successor, see: Nicham Ross, "Jewish Identity without Judaism in the Thought of Ahad Ha-am and Mordecai Kaplan," *International Journal of Jewish Education Research* 5–6 (2009): 23–51. It's worth noting that some Jewish thinkers felt that the attempt to turn Judaism into a "culture" was synthetic and illogical. One of the more prominent ones was Leo Strauss, who wrote, "Judaism cannot be understood as a culture. There are folk dances and pottery and all that. But you can't live on that. The substance is not culture, but divine revelation." See: Leo Strauss, "Why We Remain Jews: Can Jewish Faith and History Still Speak to Us?" in *Leo Strauss: Political Philosopher and Jewish Thinker*, eds. Kenneth L. Deutsch and Walter Nicgorski, Rowman & Littlefield, 1994, 52.

(The chapter is based on a lecture that Strauss delivered at the University of Chicago in 1962).

73 Aviva Aviv notes that "despite the outward similarity to Reform Jews, who also placed most of Judaism on an ethical foundation, Ahad Ha'am actually draws the essence of his worldview, and perhaps also its vitality, from the Orthodox world." See: Aviva Aviv, *Ahad Ha-am's Concept of Jewish Nationalism*, Boston Spa: British Library Document Supply Centre, 1987.

74 The complete text of the essay [in Hebrew] appears in the Ben Yehuda Project: http://benyehuda.org/ginzburg/medinat_hayehudim.html.

75 See: Rina Hevlin, *Dual Commitment: Jewish Identity Between Tradition and Secularity in Ahad Ha'am's Thought*. Sifrut Achshav, 2001, 73 [Hebrew]. Hevlin writes that Ahad Ha'am's prophecy "undergoes rationalization and reduction to a mission of justice and morality."

76 The criticism appears in Ahad Ha'am's essay "The National Morality." See the Ben Yehuda Project: http://benyehuda.org/ginzburg/hamusar_haleumi.html.

77 Morality that was not created according to the dictates of a Jewish god, but rather was formulated by the Jewish people—the most important manifestation of the people's spirit. The spirit of the people is key element in Ahad Ha'am's doctrine. "The concept of Judaism embodies everything we know about the Jewish people and the quality of its national spirit," he wrote. Jewish tradition does not stem from God, but is a product of the people's spirit." *Kol Kitvei Ahad Ha' am* [Hebrew], Dvir, 1947, 103 [Hebrew].

78 According to the historian Niall Ferguson, most thinkers who listed the major civilizations produced by human society (excluding Jewish thinkers such as Shmuel Eisenstadt), left out Judaism. See: Niall Ferguson, *Civilization: The West and the Rest*, Penguin Books, 2011, 3.

79 See: Moshe Halbertal, "Modern Jewish Identities and the State of Israel," in *Conditions for the Prosperity of the State of Israel*, Samuel Neaman Institute, 2006 [Hebrew]. Halbertal talks about how Jews with these identities interpret the historical reality of exile, which Jews experienced throughout most of their documented history. "The traditional identity viewed Jewish history as a stage where the covenant relationships materialize…Jewish nationalism…regarded exile as a state of dependence that leads to both spiritual and political demise… the cosmopolitan Jew interprets the history of exile as a tragic situation that engenders a unique moral sensitivity."

80 George Steiner is one of the most important of those thinkers. It's worth noting that Halbertal and other critics of the "cosmopolitan" Jewish stance believe that one of its problems is that in practice, it brings about the end of the Jewish people. In Steiner's case, he even expressed a certain interest in the completion of the Jewish project. For more, see Assaf Sagiv, "George Steiner's Jewish Problem," in *The Wounds of Possibility: Essays on George Steiner*, ed. Ricardo Gil Soeiro. Cambridge Scholars Publishing, 2012; and Edward Alexander and Paul Bogdanor, eds. *The Jewish Divide Over Israel: Accusers and Defenders*, Transaction Publishers, 2006.

81 The data was published by Pew in "A Portrait of Jewish Americans," chapter 3, 2013.

82 See: *A Portrait of Israeli Jews: Beliefs, Observances, and Values,* 2009. See also: "Guttmann Center for Surveys, Israel Democracy Institute and the Avi Chai Foundation," 2012, 44. The exact figures are: 80 percent believe that God exists, 67 percent believe in the chosen people, 65 percent believe in the Torah's Commandments. See also: "Israel's Religiously Divided Society," Pew, 2016. According to that report, 50 percent of the Jews in Israel believe in God "with absolute certainty" (p. 50 in the complete report).

83 The data comes from Pew, "Jewish American in 2020." In the Pew survey, the Jews are clearly treated as a religious, and perhaps also ethnic, group—but certainly not a national one. Therefore, when asked about the meaning of Judaism an option of "nationality" was not even presented to the respondents.

21 percent of the Jews said that "being Jewish is mainly a matter of ancestry," 22 percent chose "culture," and 11 percent said it was religion. Other Jews chose combinations of two or all three components.

84 Guttmann Center data: 73 percent believe that Israeli Jews and Diaspora Jews share a common destiny (73 percent said they "agree" or "totally agree"). However, more than half of the respondents (57 percent) "agree" or "totally agree" that the Jews in Israel are a different nation than the Jews abroad.

85 See: Rosner and Gil, *Jewish and Democratic: Perspectives from World Jewry*, 67. "We know the following to be established facts: A significant majority of Jews supports Israel, is emotionally attached to Israel, and regards Israel as an essential element in its Jewish identity; attachment to Israel, in all countries and for most groups, is a reliable predictor of Jewish identity levels." Additionally, according to Pew's "Jewish American in 2020" report, 58 percent of US Jews say they feel very or somewhat attached to Israel.

86 Rabbi Abraham Joshua Heschel was one the most important thinkers of American Jewry in the twentieth century. And see: Abraham Joshua Heschel, *Moral Grandeur and Spiritual Audacity: Essays*, ed. Susannah Heschel. Farrar, Straus & Giroux, 1996.

87 I heard their story while working on a newspaper story. They asked not to divulge their last name. Most children who grow up in interfaith families are raised as Jews, but without their parents telling them that they are "exclusively Jewish." See: Shmuel Rosner, "Most Children of Intermarriage Aren't Told They are Exclusively Jewish," *Jewish Journal*, 2015 (based on Theodore Sasson, et al., *Millennial Children of Intermarriage: Touchpoints and Trajectories of Jewish Engagement*. Brandeis University, Cohen Center for Modern Jewish Studies, 2015).

88 See chapter 9 of: Shaye J.D. Cohen, *The Beginnings of Jewishness: Boundaries, Varieties, Uncertainties,* University of California Press, 1999.

89 Arthur J. Wolak, "Ezra's Radical Solution to Judean Assimilation," *Jewish Bible Quarterly* 40 (April-June 2012): 95–105. The attribution of matrilineality to the days of Ezra is highly accepted and was also cited in a ruling of the Israeli Supreme Court (by Justice Silberg in the Shalit case: HC 58/68, *Benjamin Shalit, et al. v. The Minister of Interior, et al.*).

90 Mentioned in the Book of Ezra and the Book of Nehemiah: Ezra 9–10; Nehemiah, 9, 1–3; 13, 1–3; 23–30.

91 Yonina Dor, Have the 'Foreign Women' Really Been Expelled?: Separation and Exclusion in the Restoration Period, Magnes Press, 2006 [Hebrew].

92 Meir Soloveichik, "The Jewish Mother: A Theology," *Azure*, 20 (Spring 2005).

93 The Reform Movement's Resolution on Patrilineal Descent. Report of the Committee on Patrilineal Descent, adopted March 15, 1983.

94 Actually, they recognize anyone who has a Jewish parent and Jewishness is established "through appropriate and timely public and formal acts of

identification with the Jewish faith and people." For more about the subject, see Sylvia Barack Fishman, *Fathers of the Faith? Three Decades of Patrilineal Descent in American Reform Judaism*, JPPI, 2013. And see Shmuel Rosner, *Shtetl, Bagel, Baseball: On the Dreadful, Wonderful State of America's Jews*, Keter, 2011, 58–60 [Hebrew].

95 Sylvia Barack Fishman, Fathers of the Faith?, n.d., n.p.

96 For an interesting discussion about the halakhic sources of who is a Jew of matrilineal descent, and of the problem inherent in the decision of the Reform movement, see J. David Bleich, *Contemporary Halakhic Problems, vol. 3*, Ktav Publishing House, 1989, 82.

97 Here, too, it depends on who's counting and what the criteria are. See: Rosner, *Shtetl, Bagel, Baseball*, chapter 1. According to a survey conducted by Pew in 2013, there were around 6.7 million Jews in the United States that year. In 2015, Leonard Saxe, a researcher at Brandeis University, said there were 7 million. According to the Central Bureau of Statistics in Israel, that same year there were approximately 6.2 million Jews in Israel.

98 61 percent of US Jews who married after 2010 married a non-Jewish partner. The data published by Pew (2020) clearly indicates that someone with only one Jewish parent is much less likely to marry a Jewish partner than someone who has two Jewish parents. An additional analysis of the Pew data from 2013 can be found in this article: Jack Wertheimer and Steven M. Cohen, "The Pew Survey Reanalyzed: More Bad News, but a Glimmer of Hope," *Mosaic Magazine*. November 2, 2014.

99 The same allegation can, of course, also be made against those who made the decision, who by deciding to ignore the risk inherent in that decision, are in practice dividing the Jewish people.

100 For more background about the subject, see Lawrence H. Schiffman, "Jewish Identity and Jewish Descent," *Judaism* 34 (Winter, 1985): 83. With regard to the prohibition on marrying Karaites, see Michael Corinaldi, *The Personal Status of the Karaites*. Rubin Maas Publishers, 1988, 101 ff. [Hebrew]. And see n.a.,"On the History of the Karaites in the East," *Zion* 1(1936), 209 [Hebrew].

101 That claim appears in many writings that reconstruct the circumstances under which the decision was made. For example, see Norman Linzer, David J. Schnall and Jerome A. Chanes, eds. *A Portrait of the American Jewish Community*, Praeger, 1998, 152.

102 The quotes in this paragraph are from Dana Evan Kaplan, *Contemporary American Judaism: Transformation and Renewal*, Columbia University Press, 2009, 184.

103 The following paragraphs are taken from a position paper that was prepared for a JPPI conference. Sections of the paper are also incorporated into the rest of the chapter. See: Shmuel Rosner, *Conversion: After the Dialogue and the Crisis*. JPPI, 2011.

104 In this context, it's interesting to note that according to one of the explanations, the Book of Ruth was written in the days of Ezra in reaction to the decrees he imposed regarding foreign women. The Babylonian Talmud, *Yevamot*: "Rabbi Elazar said, what is the scriptural protocol. It is written, and when she saw that she was steadfastly minded to go with her, she left off speaking unto her. 'We are forbidden,' she told her, to go beyond the Sabbath boundaries.' 'Wherever thou goest, I shall go.' 'We are forbidden private meeting between man and woman.' 'Where thou find lodging, I shall lodge.' 'We have been commanded six hundred and thirteen commandments.' 'Thy people shall be my people.' 'We are forbidden idolatry.' 'And thy God is my God.' 'Four modes of death were entrusted to the Beit Din.' 'Where thou will die, I shall I die.' 'Two graveyards were place at the disposal of the Beit Din.' 'And there shall I be buried.' Presently she saw that she was steadfastly minded." And the additions: *Nazir 23:* "Daughter of the son of Eglon," "meaning that Ruth was young when she converted."

105 Steven M. Cohen, Jacob R. Ukeles, and Ron Miller, *Jewish Community Study of New York: 2011—Comprehensive Report*, UJA-Federation of New York, June 2012.

106 Steven M. Cohen, Jacob R. Ukeles, and Ron Miller, *Special Study on "Partly Jewish" Jews*. UJA-Federation of New York, November 2013. According to that study, five out of every one hundred Jews in New York in 2011 were Jews by virtue of "personal choice"—namely, Jews who don't have a Jewish parent or didn't convert. There is a high correlation between Jews by personal choice and partially Jewish Jews. About one-quarter of partly Jewish Jews (23 percent) are Jews by "personal choice," as opposed to only 2 percent of the Jews for whom Judaism is their sole religion/identity. There are researchers, such as Leonard Saxe, who believe that that the "partially" Jewish category is to a great extent the result of problematic survey questions which led Jews to provide that answer. When writing this book, Saxe was engaged in completing a study on "partial" Jews.

107 Cases of "partial-Jewish" Jews were seen under Roman rule, but they disappeared as rabbinic Judaism became more established in the period of the Exile. For more about "partly Jewish" families today, see Susan Katz Miller, *Being Both: Embracing Two Religions in One Interfaith Family*, Beacon Press, 2013; and Susan Katz Miller, "Being 'Partly Jewish,'" *The New York Times*, Oct. 31, 2013. In the comprehensive survey dealing with American Jewry conducted by Pew, around 1 million Jews were identified as being "partly" Jewish. They're "proud" to (also) be "Jewish," but observe very little "Judaism." Being Jewish is "important" to only a minority of them, but they currently have no reason to remove the Jewish component of their identity, which is one of many components. For more data about the "partially Jewish" Jews, see the chapter on demography in the JPPI's Annual Assessment for the years 2014–2015.

108 Pew, 2013.

109 For example, a group that analyzed the findings of the comprehensive study on American Jewry decided to remove those Jews "whose only connection with Judaism is a sense of shared values"—and transfer them to the "close to Judaism" group. See: Elizabeth Tighe, et al., *Recoding of Jews in the Pew Portrait of Jewish Americans*, Brandeis University American Jewish Population Project, July 9, 2014.

110 The term is used in the above-cited research by Tighe, et al.

111 In a report she submitted to the Minister of Justice, entitled *Constitutional Anchoring of Israel's Vision*, Professor Ruth Gavison wrote,: "The contexts of registration, the Law of Return, personal status and other matters are all mixed into the issue of 'Who is a Jew.' There is no uniform answer to the question 'Who is a Jew?' according to Israeli law. Often times, the context determines both the answer as well as the identity of the person providing it." See also: Ruth Gavison, *The Law of Return at Sixty Years: History, Ideology, Justification*, Metzilah Center, 2009 [Hebrew].

112 For example, the aforementioned report found that Israeli Jews "broadly agree" (92 percent of the respondents) that a person can be a good Jew even if he or she doesn't observe religious tradition.

113 Pew 2013, 8: "Secularism has a long tradition in Jewish life in America, and most U.S. Jews seem to recognize this: 62% say being Jewish is mainly a matter of ancestry and culture, while just 15% say it is mainly a matter of religion."

114 Steven M. Cohen and Kerry Olitzky, "Another Way to Join the Jewish People?," *The Forward*, December 9, 2013.

115 My colleague, Rabbi Dov Maimon, PhD, presented his proposal at the Israeli Presidential Conference 2011 in Jerusalem. His remarks can be viewed using the following link: http://jppi.org.il/uploads/FacingTomorrow2011_DovMaimon.html.

116 See: Regev Ben David, "Joining the Jewish people in light of modern Jewish sovereignty", Metzilah Center, 2018 [Hebrew].

117 Barry A. Kosmin and Ariela Keysar, "American Jewish Secularism: Jewish Life Beyond the Synagogue," in *American Jewish Year Book 2012*, ed. Arnold Dashefsky and Ira Sheskin. Springer, 2013, 3–53.

118 See: Shmuel Rosner and Dov Maimon, *Creating Change Through Diversity*, JPPI, 2012 [Hebrew].

119 See: Exploring the Jewish Spectrum in a Time of Fluid Identity, Shmuel Rosner and John Ruskay, JPPI, 2016.

120 A study by JPPI "indicates the existence of major gaps between Jewish consciousness in Israel and the kind of Jewish consciousness demonstrated by Diaspora-based studies (with an emphasis on the US). This has mainly to do with Israeli Jews' relatively strong adherence to an outlook that defines Jewishness in

terms of ethnicity, usually that of the mother." See Shmuel Rosner, Camil Fuchs, and Noah Slepkov,: *Who is a Jew: Viewpoints of Israeli Jews*, JPPI, 2023.

121 The complete correspondence appears in this book: Eliezer Ben-Rafael, *Jewish Identities: Fifty Intellectuals Answer Ben-Gurion*, Brill, 2002.

122 That survey took place in the wake of a political crisis, as described in detail in: Eliezer Don-Yehiya, "Religion, National Identity and Politics: The Crisis over the Question of 'Who is a Jew'—1958," in *On Both Sides of the Fence: Religion and State in the Early Years of Israel*, Ben Zvi Institute, 2002 [Hebrew].

123 Arrangements pertaining to immigration in the early years of the State of Israel underwent several shakeups and changes, stemming, among other things, from the fact that many interfaith couples came to the country and the State was unsure about how to treat them. For more about the discussions and debates that accompanied this matter, see : Dvora Hacohen, "The Law of Return and its Implications," in The *First Fifty Years*, ed. Anita Shapira. Zalman Shazar Center, 1998, 57–88 [Hebrew].

124 To better understand the legal context of the crisis, I made use of: Ruth Gavison, *Constitutional Anchoring of Israel's Vision*, 2013.

125 The quote is from Zerach Warhaftig, a member of the National Religious Party, and appears in Don-Yehiya.

126 See: Eitan Levontin, "A Castle in the Air: The Funk-Schlezinger Decision and Population Registry Laws, *Mishpat Umimshal* 11(1): 2007: 125–193 [Hebrew].

127 The quotes appear in Don-Yehiya.

128 According to Don-Yehiya, who disagrees with the denominational division made by Ben-Rafael.

129 Ben-Rafael.

130 Shmuel Rosner, "The Ultimate Conversion," *The New York Times* (Latitude Opinion Blog), July 9, 2013. For more about sociological conversion in Israel, also see: Alexander Yakobson, "Joining the Jewish People: Non-Jewish Immigrants from the Former USSR, Israeli Identity and Jewish Peoplehood, *The Israel Law Review* 43[1] (2009): 218–239.

131 Halbertal, "Modern Jewish Identities and the State of Israel."

132 That's what happened in 2007 when the soldier, Valentina Ivseinko, was buried in the military cemetery in Kiryat Ata. Ivseinko came to Israel from Chernobyl when she was fifteen years old, and her short life ended tragically in an automobile accident while serving in the army. After her burial, parents of other soldiers buried in the same cemetery found out that a soldier whom they believed wasn't Jewish was interred next to their children. They demanded that Ivseinko's body be moved because "non-Jews are not buried in a Jewish cemetery." Ivseinko's friends from Kibbutz Barkai, where she had lived as a lone soldier, demanded that her body remain where it was. This case, unlike that of Pesachov, ended with a victory of the halakhic position and not of "the modern consciousness

of solidarity." See: Mirit Pinhas and Nachman Gilboa, "The Restless Death of Valentina Ivseinko," *Hadaf Hayarok*, March 22, 2007 [Hebrew].

133 See: Gili Cohen, "Family of Fallen Soldier: Jewish Status Shouldn't Have Mattered in Memorial Ceremony," *Haaretz*, April 13, 2013 [Hebrew].

134 In his book, Stern describes the campaign he waged to institute friendly conversion in the IDF. See: Elazar Stern, *Navigations*, Yediot Sefarim, 2009 [Hebrew]. For more about that campaign and other campaigns that Stern waged against the rabbinical establishment, see: Shmuel Rosner, "The Red Beret and the Rabbis," *The Jewish Review of Books*, Winter 2011.

135 This tragic affair culminated with a regulation signed by the Minister of Defense. It stipulates that soldiers whose Judaism is in doubt are to be buried in lots where Jewish soldiers are also buried, but at a distance of four *amahs* (a biblical unit of measurement) from soldiers whose Judaism is not in doubt. See: Yossi Yehoshua, "An End to the Injustice: Soldiers Whose Judaism is in Doubt Will Not Be Buried Separately," *Yedioth Ahronoth*, January 2016.

136 It should be noted that an interesting reverse question can also be asked: Should a Jew who fights against the Jewish state or against the Jewish people not be considered a Jew?

137 Ben-Rafael.

138 For more about this subject, see the chapter by Shalom Ratzabi in Ben-Rafael.

139 In Oz and Oz-Salzberger, Amos Oz writes that: "A Jew, in my unhalakhic opinion, is someone who chooses to share the fate of other Jews, or who is condemned to do so."

140 Ben-Rafael. Berlin's definition is reminiscent of, but different than the one posited by the philosopher, Jean-Paul Sartre. See endnote 21 in question 1 above.

141 The dispute between Rabbi Akiva and Ben Azzai over the cardinal principle pertains to two biblical verses: (1) Leviticus 19:18: "You shall neither take revenge on nor bear a grudge against the members of your people; you shall love your neighbor as yourself;" (2) Genesis 5:1: "This is the narrative of the generations of man; on the day that God created man, in the likeness of God he created him." A different version of the dispute appears in Genesis *Rabbah:* R. Ben Azzai said, "These are the generations of Adam" is a great principle of the Torah." R. Akiva said: , "You shall love your neighbor as yourself" is a great principle of the Torah. Thus, one should not say, "Since I have been scorned, let my fellow be scorned as well; since I have been cursed, let my fellow be cursed as well." R. Tanhumah said: "If you do so, realize who it is you are willing to put to shame—"one who was made in the likeness of God." (Genesis *Rabbah* 24:7).

142 Genesis 18:23: "And Abraham came forward and said: Would you obliterate the righteous along with the wicked?"

143 See Deuteronomy 9:14: "Leave Me alone and I will destroy them and obliterate their name from the heavens, and I will make you unto a nation mightier and more numerous than they." And Moses's reaction: "And I fell down before the

Lord as before, for forty days and forty nights; I neither ate bread nor drank water, because of all your sins you had committed, by doing evil in the eyes of the Lord to anger Him."

144 For Gideon's reaction to what the angel sent to him said, see: Judges 6:13–14.

145 1 Samuel 15.

146 Babylonian Talmud *Yoma* 22.

147 See Deuteronomy 21:1–9: "If a slain person be found in the land...[and] it is not known who slew him, then...all the elders of that city, who are the nearest to the corpse, shall wash their hands over the calf that was decapitated in the valley, and they shall announce and say 'our hands did not shed this blood nor did our eyes see it done;" "Atone for Your people Israel..."

148 This version undoubtedly articulates moral discomfort with the command that Saul received. The original text says: "When the Holy One, blessed be He, said to Saul: 'Now go and smite Amalek.' He said: 'If on account of one person the Torah said to perform the ceremony of the calf who is to be decapitated, how much more for all these persons. And if a man has sinned, what sin has the beast committed; and if the adults have sinned, what have the little ones done?"

149 Exodus 32:12.

150 "Now, leave Me alone, so that My anger can be kindled against them and that I may destroy them, and I will make you in to a great nation." Exodus 32:10.

151 "Do not be overrighteous" refers to Ecclesiastes 7:16.

152 I'm refraining from an extensive discussion about the precise definition of the term "values" because it promises to be lengthy and complicated. Delving into it will require a significant digression from the subject matter of the book. I'll mention in brief that Professor Pinchas Peli suggested making a distinction between the "principles of Judaism" and the "values of Judaism" so that principles are "ideas, beliefs and opinions from which I come and go," whereas values are "ideas, beliefs and opinions to and towards I go." See: Pinchas Peli, "In An Attempt to Formulate the Principles of Judaism for Contemporary Times," *Amudim* 32 (1984) [Hebrew]. In this chapter, I chose to focus on an even more limited scope pertaining to the question of how Jews, in their daily lives, adapt themselves to behavior which they identify as being ethical, moral and of the kind that is consistent with their natural interpretation of what can be called "values." And it's worth adding: with regard to the question of what "values" are as opposed to what "morality" is—let's decide that for the sake of this discussion, morality is a system of values that serve as an ideal which human beings strive to achieve in their behavior. In the course of the chapter we make use of the terms morality and values interchangeably when meaning a similar thing. However, there are certain places where the natural understanding of morality and of values is not identical. For instance: if literacy is a Jewish "value," it's not clear that it has a connection with "morality."

153 That question, as well as the other questions discussed, cannot of course be divorced from what was discussed in the chapter dealing with "What is Judaism?"—is there a rigid "Judaism" which is not dependent on what Jews practice in a certain period, or is there a "Judaism" that's entirely about what Jews do in a certain period. See also: Yehuda Shaviv, "Divine Torah as Opposed to Human Morality According to Rabbi Abraham Isaac Kook," *Sinai* 117 (1995) [Hebrew} and: Avi Sagi, *Between Religion and Morality*, Hakibbutz Hameuchad, 1998 [Hebrew].

154 This is a somewhat simplistic presentation of Leibowitz's doctrine, due to lack of space. For more about the subject, see: Michael Ohana, "The Perception of Morality in Yeshayahu Leibowitz's Educational-Religious Thought," *Iyun VeMehkar BeHachsharat Morim* 10 (2006), 181–190 [Hebrew]. Ohana writes: "Morality, as an expression of the spirit of man that guides him according to his obligation or according to his perception of reality, is, in Leibowitz's opinion, an atheist-humanist category which places man, and not God, at its center. Therefore, as he sees it, such morality cannot be extracted from the sources of Judaism, which sees and recognizes the obligation to do 'the right thing before God, and not the right thing before man.'" The quote from Leibowitz is from: *Torah and the Commandments in Our Time*, Massada, 1954, 143 [Hebrew]. Compared to that view, it's worth proposing, at least as an endnote, the view which posits that Jewish moral values that rely on the Torah and the Prophets are not a product of divine guidance, but rather of human nature (or as the researcher David Novak puts it—natural law), and for that reason are universal moral values. He expands on this subject in *Natural Law in Judaism*.

155 Leibowitz, Torah and the Commandments in Our Time, 11.

156 See: Naomi Kasher, *Leibowitz and Kant: Being Moral or Not Being Religious* [Hebrew]. This was a lecture delivered at a conference marking the one hundredth anniversary of Leibowitz's birth, held at Ben-Gurion University of the Negev, 2003. Kasher says, "Leibowitz neither wants to or can deny that religious Jews, himself included, have goals and interests apart from worshipping God. However, their religiosity will be articulated by always giving priority to the inner religious value, which is an end in itself. In other words, in their world worshipping God will have priority over all the other values which don't have inner value, but rather are founded on the needs and inclinations of the person who holds them to be true."

157 In his book *Moses's Final Speech*, Micah Goodman talks about different patterns of human response to the clash between conscience and the biblical narrative, and mentions three major patterns: fundamentalism—ethical surrender to the biblical texts and to what they say; anachronism—creative interpretation; quandary—choosing to live in a state of inner conflict: "To experience the painful gap between morality and the Bible," 177–186.

158 Zvi Arad, *Jewish Values, The Biblical Background*, Machbarot Lesifrut, 18 [Hebrew]. Based on a series of lectures delivered at the Hebrew University of Jerusalem.

159 With regard to the sanctity of life, many commentators rely on the Torah portion *Acharei Mot.* It contains a verse which establishes a general directive governing the fulfillment of the Commandments: "…which a man shall do and live by them." (Leviticus 18:5). The Talmud (*Yoma* 85b) stipulates: "…and shall live by them, and not die by them." The value of human life prevails over the value of fulfilling the Commandments (apart from three prohibitions: idolatry, bloodshed, and incest).

160 Deuteronomy 25:19.

161 It's interesting to compare the interpretations provided by Rabbi Soloveitchik, who sees in Abraham's submission to the sacrifice demand an experience "rooted in suffering and anxiety," and by Rabbi Kook, who sees a "tranquility" in Abraham as he goes, head held high, to make the sacrifice. The comparison can perhaps teach us that Rabbi Soloveitchik assumes that Abraham was torn between his human values and his complete faith in God, whereas Rabbi Kook assumes that Abraham's faith in God is the ultimate value nesting in him. See: Rabbi Joseph B. Soloveitchik, *Divrei Hashkafa [Hebrew],* and Rabbi Abraham Isaac Kook, *Olat Reiya* [Hebrew]. Commentators have of course addressed the question of why Abraham chose to plead with God in order to spare Sodom, but surrendered to the demand to make the sacrifice without saying a word. The answer that is found in many of the writings dealing with this subject talks about Abraham's personal interest in the sacrifice matter. Because he knew he had a conflict of interest, he didn't think he was the right person to conduct the debate over the command to sacrifice Isaac.

162 Naturally, another possibility exists: that there are universal values which should not, per se, be defined as "Jewish" and actually clash with the dictates of Judaism or the Torah. We are not exploring that possibility because this chapter deals with the question of "What are Jewish Values" and not with the question of "how a decent person should behave."

163 Decisions that soften or override Torah-based dictates concerning different matters, which could lead to clashes with a person's conscience, have been made throughout history by commentators of Jewish tradition. For further reading, see: Moshe Halbertal, *Commentary Revolutions in the Making: Values as Interpretative Considerations in Midreshei Halakhah*. Magnes Press, 1997 [Hebrew]. And in the explicit context of biblical commands pertaining to human life, see: Jonathan Sacks, *Not in God's Name: Confronting Religious Violence*, Schocken Books, 2015. Sacks posits that later commentaries which actually revoked commands to use violence are not at odds with the Torah, but rather extract its true intention from it. He believes that Judaism, followed by Christianity (but not yet Islam), attained the level of understanding needed

for restraining the violence described in the Holy Scriptures when they found themselves "using it against members of their own people." In this regard, it's also worth assessing the degree to which ideas about compassion and helping the weak, whose origin is Christianity, had an effect on Judaism.

164 Samuel Hugo Bergmann, *Heaven and Earth*, Shdemot, 1969, 26 [Hebrew]. And: Samuel Hugo Bergmann, "Contraction and Expansion in Jewish Ethics," *Mahanaim* 100 (Tishri-Heshvan, 1966) [Hebrew].

165 This issue is especially prominent in Israel today, where the term "Jewish values" is often understood to mean a code that articulates a stronger religious-nationalist worldview at the expense of a Western-liberal one. See, for example, how Member of Knesset Zehava Galon reacted to the appointment of Naftali Bennett (a religious-nationalist) as Minister of Education: "Infuriating data were published last year, according to which the Ministry of Education invested NIS 56 million in organizations engaged in teaching Jewish values, as opposed to only NIS 5.5 million in those which impart democratic values. It's painful and frightening to imagine how those numbers will look next year if Naftali Bennett is in fact appointed." See: Zehava Galon, "Bennett as Minister of Education—That's Really Bad News, in Zeev Kam, *Makor Rishon*, April 2015 [Hebrew].

166 Isaac Bashevis Singer, A Young Man in Search of Love, n.d., n.p.

167 The most famous incident relating to the voice from heaven appears in the story about the Oven of Akhnai in *Bava Metzia* 59b. In contrast to that incident is the one that divided Hillel and Shammai, where "a heavenly voice declared 'the words of both schools are the words the living God, but the law follows Beit Hillel'" (*Eruvin* 13b). Talmudic commentators provide lengthy explanations about this contradiction, but it seems that both the Talmud itself (see, for instance, *Temura* 16a), as well as the halakhists, are inclined to reject the use of a heavenly voice and prefer a human authority.

168 For a comprehensive discussion dealing with the status of women in Judaism and different opinions about the way in which that status should be refashioned, see Susannah Heschel, ed., *On Being a Jewish Feminist: A Reader*, Schocken Books, 1983. Of particular interest are the chapters which present a kind of dispute between two engaging thinkers over the root of the problem that needs to be resolved for contemporary Jewish women: Cynthia Ozick, "Notes Toward Finding the Right Question," 120–151, and Judith Plaskow, "The Right Question is Theological," 223–233.

169 A single paragraph cannot do justice to the scope and force of the revolution in the role of women throughout the Jewish world. For further reading, see, for example, Pamela Nadell, *Women Who Would Be Rabbis: A History of Women's Ordination 1889–1995*, Beacon Press, 1998. And see Tamar Ross, *Expanding the Palace of Torah: Feminism and Orthodoxy*, Brandeis University Press, 2004.

170 Reliance on common texts as a source of authority characterizes Judaism more than shared values. Sources that broke with accepted norms, such as The

Zohar, still relied on those same textual sources of authority, as illustrated by Gershom Scholem. Those sources, and first and foremost the Torah, do not define clear norms of behavior, but establish the accepted scope of the discourse dealing with the norms. See: Michael Fishbane, *Biblical Interpretation in Ancient Israel*, Clarendon Press, 1985; and Michael Fishbane, *Judaism: Revelation and Traditions*, Harper and Row, 1987.

171 For more about the issue of slavery, see: Haim Cohn, *Human Rights in the Bible and the Talmud*, Ministry of Defense, The University on the Air, 1989, chapter 7 [Hebrew]. And also: Rachel Gershuni, "Hebrew Slavery Laws: An Expression of Human Dignity," *Gilyonot Parashat Hashavua* 134, Jerusalem; Ministry of Justice [Hebrew]. For more about how the values of Judaism can be reconciled with the command to fulfill the Commandments, see: Haim Sabato, "A Study of the Sources," in *Derekh Erez: Religion and State*, ed. Amichai Berholtz, Ministry of Education and Beit Morasha of Jerusalem, 2002 [Hebrew]. In the past, numerous historians recorded the fact that Jews, throughout history, were forced to lead a life of compliance with Jewish law, without having any say in the matter. See, for example: Yirmiyahu Yovel, *Dark Riddle: Hegel, Nietzsche and the Jews*, Penn State University Press, 1998, 198. An attempt, with only limited success, to assert that religious coercion cannot be reconciled with Jewish tradition was made by Moses Mendelssohn. See his preface (1782) to the German translation of the book *Vindication of the Jews* by Manasseh ben Israel.

172 Remembering the Holocaust is the number one mission of the Jews, at least according to the study conducted by Pew in 2013, (op. cit.), chapter 3. There are quite a few drawbacks and critics of this attempt to turn the Holocaust into the centerpiece of framing Jewish identity. See, for example: Avi Sagi, "The Holocaust and the Foundation of Jewish Identity," *Azure* 42 (2010).

173 See: Moshe Reis, "The Principle of Education in Judaism," *Machshevet* 25 (1971) [Hebrew]; and Yoram Rabin, *The Right to Education*, Nevo, 2001 [Hebrew]. Jewish tradition imposes an obligation on parents to educate their children.

174 Quite a few of those values are examined in detail by Yehuda Brandes in his book *Judaism and Human Rights*, IDI Press, 2013, 174 [Hebrew]. Brandes posits that there is a deep connection "between the basic values of the Torah and the modern thinking about human rights." For further reading, see Daniel Breslauer, *Judaism and Human Rights in Contemporary Thought*, Greenwood Press, 1993.

175 Leviticus 26:37; Babylonian Talmud 39a.

176 The quote is from Dubnow, 54.

177 Daniel J. Elazar, *Jewish Values in the Jewish State.* This was a paper prepared for the project: "Israel at 2020: Master Plan for Israel in the 21st Century," Jerusalem Center for Public Affairs, 1996; and see also, Brandes, *Judaism and Human Rights*: "The ideological foundation of liberalism and humanism… which were nurtured by the Bible and later sources of religious texts, including

both Christianity and Judaism." For more about the difficulty to reconcile liberal values with Judaism, see Allan Arkush's discussion of the book *Jerusalem* by Moses Mendelssohn: Allan Arkush, "The Liberalism of Moses Mendelssohn," in *The Cambridge Companion to Modern Jewish Philosophy*, ed. Michael L. Morgan and Peter Eli Gordon, Cambridge University Press, 2007, 35. The contention that "much of the conservative way of thinking—and especially when it comes to family and morality—is itself rooted in Hebraic ideas," can be found in Eric Cohen, "The Spirit of Jewish Conservatism," *Mosaic Magazine*, April 6, 2015.

178 See: Hillel Gershuni, "Is the Welfare State Jewish?" *Mida*, August 2, 2015. Gershuni talks about a number of areas where the approach and values underlying the modern welfare state diverge from the principles of Jewish law governing the obligation to help the less fortunate.

179 See, for example,: Ronald Pies, "Jewish Ethics: Hillel and Shammai Weigh in on Gun Rights, *Moment Magazine*, February 26, 2013. He concludes decisively that "poorly-regulated gun possession is dangerous and inconsistent with Jewish values." For an interesting discussion about the principles associated with this matter, from which it is possible to infer implications regarding the question of the right to bear arms, see: Elishai ben Yitzhak, "Raising Dogs and its Legal Aspects," *Gilyonot Parashat Hashavua* 192. Jerusalem; Ministry of Justice [Hebrew].

180 For more about the disqualification of parties running for the Knesset, see: Michal Shamir and Keren Margel, "Perceived Threat and Disqualification of Political Party Lists and Candidates for the Knesset: From Yardor to the 2003 Elections," *Mishpat Umimshal* 8(1) (2005): 119–154 [Hebrew].

181 The disqualification relied on the Yardor decision: *E.A. 1/65 Yardor v. Chairman of the Central Elections Committee for the Sixth Knesset, 19 P.D. III 365.* For further reading about this subject, see Ruth Gavison, "20 Years to the Yardor Decision: The Right to be Elected and the Lessons of History," in *Eighty to Shimon Agranat*, eds. Ruth Gavison and Mordechai Kremnitzer. Hebrew University of Jerusalem, 1986 [Hebrew].

182 For more about how the discussion evolved, see: Gavison, *Constitutional Anchoring of Israel's Vision*, 85 ff. The Knesset enacted the new article about a year after Kahane began serving as one of its members, and not coincidentally of course. The members of the Knesset didn't want him as their partner in the legislature.

183 That insight is discussed in detail in an extensive research study I was part of: Rosner and Gil, *Jewish and Democratic: Perspectives from World Jewry.* JPPI, 2014. Furthermore, according to a 2016 Pew study called "Israel's Religiously Divided Society," 2016, a majority of Israeli Jews (76 percent) believe that a Jewish state and democracy are compatible.

184 Benny Porat and Aviezer Ravitzky, eds. *Reflections on Jewish Democracy*, Am Oved, 2010. Written in collaboration with the Israel Democracy Institute [Hebrew].

185 Alon Gal, "About Israel, the Diaspora and Zionist Democracy, in *Iyunim Bitkumat Israel*, 14 (2004): 509–536 [Hebrew].

186 Achrei Rabim LeHatot. Yair Sheleg. Following the Multitude: Rabbinic Attitudes Towards Democracy, Israel Democracy Institute, 2006 [Hebrew].

187 This is what Rabbi Yoel Bin-Nun believes. See: Yoel Bin-Nun, "A Democratic Regime According to the Torah," in *Derekh Erez: Religion and State*, ed. Amichai Berholtz, Ministry of Education and Beit Morasha of Jerusalem, 2002 [Hebrew].

188 Pew, "A Portrait of Jewish Americans," 2013, 14. Jews in Israel have different views on this subject: Pew, *Israel's Religiously Divided Society*, 2016, See also: Robert P. Jones and Daniel Cox, *2012 Jewish Values Survey: Chosen for What?* Washington, DC: Public Religion Research Institute, 2012. In that survey, American Jewish respondents ranked a large number of values which they attach great importance to—84 percent cited pursuing justice, 72 percent *tikkun olam*, and 72 percent welcoming the stranger. An extensive discussion about *tikkun olam* and its standing among American Jewry today can be found in Rosner, *Shtetl, Bagel, Baseball*. 95 ff.

189 American Jewish Heritage Month is celebrated every year in the United States. The full text of the President Obama's remarks can be found on the White House website: https://www.whitehouse.gov/the-press-office/2015/05/22/remarks-president-jewish-american-heritage-month.

190 The intimations appeared in the speech, but even more in other comments Obama made during the months of controversy over the 2015 nuclear deal with Iran.

191 See: Remarks by President Biden and Second Gentleman Douglas Emhoff at a Celebration for Jewish American Heritage Month, May 20, 2024.

192 For more about Obama and the impact of "Jewish values" on his worldview, see, among others: David Remnick, *The Bridge: The Life and Rise of Barack Obama*, Knopf, 2010. I also dealt with the subject of Obama and Jewish values in my book: Rosner, *Shtetl, Bagel, Baseball*, 106 ff. For more about the strange history of the Judeo-Christian concept in the United States, see: Gene Zubovich, "The Short Strange Career of Judeo-Christianity," *Aeon*, March 2016.

193 A quote by the researcher Charles Liebman, which is cited in: Jonathan D. Sarna, "The Cult of Synthesis in American Jewish Culture," *Jewish Social Studies* 5 (Fall 1998/Winter 1999): 52–79.

194 Arnold M. Eisen, *The Chosen People in America: A Study in Jewish Religious Ideology*, Indiana University Press, 1983. Similar acts of assimilation that necessitated a reexamination of key values can also be found in other communities over the generations. For instance, the members of the Grand Sanhedrin—Assembly of Jewish Notables, who convened in France in 1806 further to a decree by Napoleon, decided to revoke the prohibition on Jews marrying non-Jews (the Sanhedrin did however stress that the newly permissible form of marriage was not according to the religion of Moses and Israel). Something

similar occurred in Germany in the nineteenth century at an assembly of rabbis from the Reform movement.

195 See: Jonathan Sacks, *Radical Then, Radical Now: Exploring the Legacy of the World's Oldest Religion*, The Free Press, 2000, 55. According to Sacks, "Judaism is a uniquely restless faith." In other words, it's a persistent opposition to the prevailing fashion.

196 See: Steven M. Cohen and Lauren Blitzer, "Belonging Without Believing: Jews and their Distinctive Patterns of Religiosity—and Secularity: Selected Results from the 2008 Pew Forum U.S. Religious Landscape Survey," FGH/JCC Association Research Center, 2008. The researchers write that "Jews are the most liberal, most tolerant on social issues, and least favorable to religious influence in the political domain."

197 For more about this subject, see: Rosner and Maimon. Among other things, the paper proposes the following distinction: "When comparing young American Jews and young Israeli Jews, what stand out first are lines of difference in the main components of Jewish identity…in this discourse, it appears that the Jewish community in Israel fills the role of the modern equivalent of the Jerusalem community—ethnic Judaism—whereas the American Jewish community plays the role of the modern equivalent of the Alexandrian community—ethical Judaism. The different circumstances mentioned above are what drove the two communities to react in an opposite manner and draw opposite conclusions (a 'defensive' ethnic reaction as opposed to an 'involved' ethical reaction) as a result of past traumas in Jewish history."

198 Obama did it when he spoke about how Jewish values require him to think about a "Palestinian child in Ramallah that feels trapped without opportunity."

199 See: "What's a Jewish State in Your Opinion? The Leaders Reply," *Makor Rishon*, May 2014 [Hebrew].

200 See: Aryeh Deri, "We Have No Choice—We Have to Form a National Unity Government," *Calcalist*, September 2011 [Hebrew].

201 See: Maimonides, *Laws of Gifts to the Poor, 7:10.* "If a person refuses to give charity, or gives less than is proper for him, he must be compelled by the court to comply until he gives…" The community's power of coercion, particularly in the days of the exile, was a subject of significant discussion in different periods. Rabbi Asher Bar Yechiel grappled with it at the beginning of the 14th century, when he was presented with a case in which the community asked to execute "a difficult person"—the assumption being that if the execution was not carried out, the practical consequences for the community would be much worse. See: Benjamin Rabinowitz Teomim, "Mishpatei Nefashot BeDin HaSanhedrin uVeDin HaMalkhut," *HaTorah VeHaMedinah* 4 (1952): 46, 78. Ibid. 47, 79.

202 The Ministry of Social Affairs and Social Services website: http://molsa.gov.il/focus/pages/focusdetails.aspx?listid=feef17b7-63c7-454c-a36f-

c8d3bcb5e288&webid=16877ef1-d635-43df-a851-3a73ddbd0ab3&itemid=9 [Hebrew].

203 The quote is from: Yehuda Bar Shalom, "In the Path of Protestantism," *Haaretz*, December 2004.[Hebrew]. The German Jewish philosopher Hermann Cohen viewed socialism as a key value that derives from Jewish culture. His student Franz Rosenzweig wrote that in a certain period in Cohen's life, the only bridge between him and Jewish tradition was socialism. See: Andrea Poma, "Hermann Cohen: Judaism and Critical Idealism," in Michael L. Morgan and Peter Eli Gordon, 83.

204 See Hillel Gershuni. And also: Joseph Isaac Lifshitz, *Judaism, Law & The Free Market: An Analysis*, Acton Institute, 2012. It's also worth reading about the interesting debate whether price regulation is an obligation deriving from Jewish sources. See: Aaron Levine, *Economic Morality and Jewish Law*, Oxford University Press, 2012, chap. 4. Rabbi The Lord Jonathan Sacks also addressed the matter of the economic principles of Judaism in: Jonathan Sacks, *Markets and Morals*, Institute of Economic Affairs, 1999. The publication is based on the Seventh Annual IEA Hayek Memorial Lecture that Sacks delivered in London on June 2, 1998.

205 The quotes about moral sensitivity and the differentiation from other peoples appear in Micah Goodman, "Judaism's Zionist Opportunity," *Makor Rishon*, October 2015 [Hebrew] and Amnon Dokov, "Humanistic Judaism Also Needs to Make Room for God," *Makor Rishon*, November 2015 [Hebrew].

206 In 2015, I headed an extensive research study by the JPPI that dealt with Jewish values and Israel's use of force. (See: Shmuel Rosner and Michael Herzog, "Jewish Values and Israel's Use of Force in Armed Conflict: Perspectives from World Jewry," JPPI, 2015.). I have made use of that report in this section of the current chapter.

207 Just like any politics of defense policy which "is inescapably informed by values, Jewish politics must be informed by Jewish values" as well, says the researcher Yehudah Mirsky. See: Yehudah Mirsky, "The Political Morality of Pacifism and Nonviolence: One Jewish View, in *War and its Discontents*, ed. J. Patout Burns. Georgetown University Press, 1996, 47–66, and Charles Liebman, who wrote about Israel's secular Jews: Charles Liebman, "The Culture Wars in Israel: A New Mapping," in *State in the Making: Israeli Society in the First Decades*, ed. Anita Shapira. Zalman Shazar Center, 2001, 256 [Hebrew].

208 Ruth Wisse, *Jews and Power*, Schocken Books, 2007.

209 Joseph Isaac Lifshitz, "War and Aesthetics in Jewish Law," in *War and Peace in Jewish Tradition: From the Ancient World to Present*, eds. Yigal Levin and Amnon Shapira. Routledge, 2012, 103–115.

210 See: Yehuda Amital, "The Wars of Israel According to Maimonides," *Tehumim* 5(1987), 460 [Hebrew] and Aviezer Ravitzky, "Prohibited Wars in the Jewish

Tradition," in *The Ethics of War and Peace; Religious and Secular Perspectives*, ed. Terry Nardin. Princeton University Press, 1996, 115–127.

211 See: Moshe Hellinger, "War and Peace in Jewish Tradition: Between Idealism and Realism," in *War and Peace*, ed. Shlomo Avineri, Zalman Shazar Center, 2010, 73–98 [Hebrew].

212 Even the authority to declare war remains vague. Jewish sources make reference to the "king" or the "Sanhedrin"—two institutions which disappeared many centuries ago. Whether a contemporary ethical authority exists that can fill their role also from a halakhic perspective—like the Government of Israel or the Israeli Knesset—is an open question. See: Rosner and Herzog.

213 This pertains to two-thirds of the Jews in Israel. In this survey, most of them (71 percent) said that "they live in accordance with Jewish values." See: Israel Democracy Institute and the Avi Chai Foundation, *A Portrait of Israeli Jews: Beliefs, Observances, and Values.*

214 The question was asked in a survey that was part of the research for Dr. Micah Goodman's book *The Eighth Day*, n.p., 2023 [Hebrew].

215 See: Rosner and Herzog. One of the research questions we asked the survey participants had four answers for them to choose from. The breakdown of the responses was as follows: "Jewish values demand a higher level of moral conduct in armed conflict than stipulated in international law"—40 percent; "Jewish values offer a different interpretation of morality in armed conflict situations compared to international law—33 percent; "Jewish values demand a lower level of moral conduct in armed conflict than stipulated in international law—0.4 percent; "There is no such thing as accepted 'Jewish values' when thinking about the prosecution of armed conflict"—26.5 percent.

216 Professor Shalom Rosenberg refuses to view this quote as a difference of opinion. "It seems to me that there is no disagreement between them, but rather Ben Azzai wants to complement Rabbi Akiva's principle." See: Shalom Rosenberg, "A Cardinal Principle in the Torah," *Makor Rishon*, April 2015 [Hebrew].

217 I found this interpretation in a short sermon delivered by Rabbi Yitzhak Bart (http://etzion.org.il/vbm/archive/yomyom/f/fl8.php) [Hebrew]. Based on this sermon, It's interesting to compare Rabbi Akiva's position (the obligation position) with his position concerning the verse "your brother should live with you" (Leviticus 25:36), about which Rabbi Akiva said: "your life takes precedence over the life of your friend' (*Bava Metzia* 62a). Some consider this a reflection of "the debate over whether there are 'human rights' in Judaism or just obligations." Ostensibly, *Bava Metzia* provides proof that "according to Rabbi Akiva, there is a right to life and it takes precedence over the obligation towards the other person." (See: Brandes, 72, Note 66). Rabbi Benny Lau offered another interesting interpretation regarding this debate. He argues that Ben Azzai is referring to the relationship between a man and woman. See: Binyamin Lau, "The Sanctity Between One Person and Another," *Haaretz*, 2007 [Hebrew].

218 The Talmud tells a story about a Gentile who comes to Shammai and says to him: "Convert me to Judaism on the condition that you teach me the entire Torah while I'm standing on one foot." Shammai refused and drove the man away with the builder's cubit that he had in his hand. The Gentile then approached Hillel with the same request. Hillel agreed to do so and encapsulated the Torah in one precept: "What is hateful to you, do not do to others." Babylonian Talmud, Tractate Shabbat 31a.

219 The biblical verse describes Jacob and Esau's meeting: "And Esau ran toward him and embraced him, and he fell on his neck and kissed him, and they wept." And Rashi interprets it as follows: "Rabbi Shimon ben Yochai said: 'It is a well-known law (halakha) that Esau hates Jacob. But his compassion overwhelmed him at that moment and he kissed him with all his heart,'" (source: *Sifrei BeHa'alotecha*). In the Sifrei manuscript, however, it's written differently: "It is not known that Esau hates Jacob." According to Menahem Kahana, printers may have abbreviated the Hebrew text and inadvertently caused later readers to replace the word "no" with the word "law." See: Menahem Kahana, *Prolegomena to a New Edition of the Sifre on Numbers*, Magnes Press, 1982, 32 [Hebrew].

220 The quote is from the most current and comprehensive book dealing with the William of Norwich blood libel, E. M. Rose, *The Murder of William of Norwich: The Origins of the Blood Libel in Medieval Europe*, Oxford University Press, 2015, 14.

221 The monk's account is the primary source of information about the affair. See: Augustus Jessop and M.R. James, eds. and trans. *The Life and Miracles of St William of Norwich by Thomas of Monmouth*, Cambridge University Press, 2011. (First published in 1896).

222 In keeping with the image of the Christ Child on the cross. See: Anthony Bale, *The Jew in the Medieval Book: English Antisemitism 1350–1500*, Cambridge University Press, 2006, 128.

223 See: Edmund Levin, *A Child of Christian Blood: Murder and Conspiracy in Tsarist Russia: The Beilis Blood Libel*, Schocken Books, 2014. The Beilis affair is the basis of Bernard Malamud's best known novel, *The Fixer*. Beilis's grandson accused Malamud of plagiarizing his grandfather's memoirs.

224 For more about the La Guardia blood libel, see: Alan Dundes, ed. *The Blood Libel Legend: A Casebook in Anti-Semitic Folklore*, University of Wisconsin Press, 1991.

225 In 1840, prominent members of the Jewish community in Damascus were accused on abducting and murdering a Capuchin monk and his Muslim servant in order to use their blood to bake matzos.

226 "The Czar on Trial," *The New York Times*, October 9, 1913.

227 The Nazi party newspaper devoted a series of articles to the subject in 1926. See: Edmund Levin, op cit.

228 See: Jonathan Frankel, The Damascus Affair: "Ritual Murder," Politics and the Jews in 1840, Cambridge University Press, 1997.

229 Rose, op cit.

230 Sanford Shepard, "The Present State of Ritual Crime in Spain," in Dundes, op cit., 166–167.

231 The quote is from: Dubnow, 137.

232 See: Peter Schafer, *Judeophobia: Attitudes toward the Jews in the Ancient World*, Harvard University Press, 1998. Assaf Sagiv noted that, contrary to what many think, "even a cursory historical survey will show that the dominant and most popular form of antisemitism derived precisely from universal paradigms, which could not be reconciled with Jewish particularism." See: Assaf Sagiv, "The Secret Passion of the New Antisemitism," *Azure* 45 (2011). While Jews didn't blend in with pagan culture, it's important to note that they also didn't reject it altogether. See: Martin Hengel, *Judaism and Hellenism: Studies in their Encounter in Palestine during the Early Hellenistic Period*, 2 vols. trans. John Bowden, Fortress Press, 1974.

233 See: Simha Goldin, *The Ways of Jewish Martyrdom*, trans. Yigal Levin and ed. C. Michael Copeland, Brepols, 2008. In his book, Goldin describes at length the sweeping justification that was given after the fact to the acts of martyrs. It's worth noting that some researchers believe there is a connection between the early blood libels in the Christian world and the killing of Jewish children by their parents during the Rhineland massacres. See: Israel Jacob Yuval, *Two Nations in Your Womb*, Am Oved, 2000 [Hebrew]. And: Yehuda Razhabi, "Yemenite Jews and Martyrdom," *Mahanaim* 41 [Hebrew].

234 Haym Soloveitchik, "Religious Law and Change: The Medieval Ashkenazic Example," *AJS Review* 12 (Fall 1987): 205–221. And: Jeffrey Woolf, *Martyrs in Hell: Immanuel of Rome on the Suicides of 1096*, For a link to the article: http://barilan.academia.edu/JeffreyWoolf.

235 The main elements of the story can be found in: David Nirenberg, *Anti-Judaism: The Western Tradition*, W. W. Norton, 2013, 40 ff. The primary source of the story was provided by Flavius Josephus in his book *Against Apion.* According to Jonathan Price in his introduction to the Hebrew edition of The War of the Jews Against the Romans (Carmel, 2009), *Against Apion* "contains some details of a personal nature," and its purpose was to "defend the Jewish people against its slanderers." (see p. 47).

236 Nirenberg, 41.

237 Freud's discussion of the issue is, of course, more elaborate. See: Sigmund Freud, *Moses and Monotheism*. It includes, for example, the assertion that some Christians hate Jews because of their own hatred of Christianity, which was forced upon them. For more about the subject, see: Richard J. Bernstein, *Freud and the Legacy of Moses*, Cambridge University Press, 1998, 75–89. For a brief discussion about psychological processes associated with antisemitism,

see: Avner Falk, "Collective Psychological Processes in Anti-Semitism," *Jewish Political Studies Review* 18:1–2 (Spring 2006).

238 Jonathan Sacks, "The Return of Anti-Semitism," *Wall Street Journal*, January 30, 2015.

239 Karl Marx wrote against the Jews and Judaism on several occasions, using blunt language that conveyed more than a hint of hatred. However, there is no wall-to-wall consensus that Marx was antisemitic as we understand the term today. See: Yoav Peled, "From Theology to Sociology: Bruno Bauer and Karl Marx on the Question of Jewish Emancipation," *History of Political Thought* 13:3 (1992), 463–485. And: Zvi Rosen, "Was Karl Marx Anti-Semitic?" *Haaretz* (June 2013) [Hebrew]. Obviously, it's worth recalling that some of the leaders of the communist revolution were Jewish.

240 Amos Elon, The Pity of it All: A History of the Jews in Germany, 1743–1933, Metropolitan Books, 2002.

241 Timothy Snyder offers an innovative approach to understanding Hitler's worldview: Timothy Snyder, *Black Earth: The Holocaust as History and Warning*, Tim Duggan Books, 2015. According to Snyder, Hitler was not an extreme nationalist. On the contrary. He viewed the state itself as a Jewish invention and sought to promote a racial struggle that extended well beyond the borders of the state. For a summary of Snyder's insights, see: Shmuel Rosner, "The Black Earth Exchange," *Jewish Journal* (October 2015). Researchers disagree about when Hitler first became antisemitic. Some believe he was already antisemitic when he spent time in Vienna, whereas others believe he became an antisemite later on in Munich. See: Peter Ross Range, *1924: The Year That Made Hitler*, Little, Brown, 2016, 14.

242 I drew my comparison between Shylock and Fagin from Hertzberg and Hirt-Manheimer, 180–185. The researchers of those works of literature may not all agree with that comparison. See the following endnote.

243 As noted above, that's how Hertzberg viewed Fagin. There are differing opinions about whether Dickens was antisemitic. For an interesting discussion about this subject, see: Edgar Johnson, "Dickens, Fagin, and Mr. Riah: The Intention of the Novelist," *Commentary* 9 (January 1950), 47–50.

244 This quote is from: Avinoam Yuval-Naeh, "Jewish Crime in 18th Century London and its Image in Popular Literature," master's thesis, Hebrew University of Jerusalem [Hebrew].

245 This comparison was taken from an article by A.B. Yehoshua, who presented it not as an affirmation, but as a question (Is there a connecting line?). See: A.B. Yehoshua, "An Attempt to Identify the Root Cause of Antisemitism," *Azure* 32 (2008). Seneca believed the Jews were lazy. Wagner claimed they lacked creativity.

246 The quote is from Talmon, 279.

247 Lazare's first quote is from Wieseltier. The second quote is from the English edition of Bernard Lazare, *Antisemitism: Its History and Causes*, http://www.vho.org/aaargh/fran/livres2/LAZeng.pdf. In his article, Wieseltier cites Lazare as having had a significant impact on Hannah Arendt's similar views, which were published in much later works (Lazare wrote at the time of the Dreyfus Affair, whereas Arendt wrote during and following the Holocaust).
248 From a speech delivered at the Austrian Union of Israelites in November 1896. It appears in: *Before Nation and World 1*, Zionist Library, 1961 [Hebrew].
249 Numerous sources cite cases of statements that are antisemitic in tone and content that were made by the heads of the Zionist movement. See, for example: Shmuel Almog, *Nationalism, Zionism, Antisemitism: Essays and Studies.* Zionist Library and Bialik Institute, 1992 [Hebrew].
250 Wieseltier, "Understanding Anti-Semitism."
251 Book of Esther, 3:8.
252 Talmon, op cit.
253 Bernard Lewis, *The Jews of Islam*, Princeton University Press, 1984, 103.
254 According to a study conducted by Pew, 73 percent of American Jews feel that way—it was the leading category chosen by the respondents, which also exceeded most of the other categories by a wide margin. For a brief summary, see: Becka A. Alpher, "70 Years After WWII, the Holocaust is Still Very Important to American Jews," *Fact Tank*, Pew, August 13, 2015.
255 Robert Liberles, *Salo Wittmayer Baron: Architect of Jewish History*. NYU Press, 1995. For a shorter version, see: Michael Stanislawski, "Salo Wittmayer Baron: Demystifying Jewish History," *Columbia* (Winter 2005–2006): 45–48.
256 In writing about the Holocaust, Baron said that "the results of the destruction continue to be felt until today, and there's no doubt whatsoever that they will be felt for decades to come, perhaps entire generations." Source: Salo Baron, "The Jewish People Before and After the Holocaust," *Mahanaim* 9, 1995 [Hebrew].
257 Dubnow, 68.
258 Paul Johnson, 236.
259 For example: in his book about the Damascus Affair, Jonathan Frankel explores at length to what extent "the blood libel stimulated Jewish national sentiment and even gave rise to a proto-Zionist movement." See page 25.
260 For more about the motivations for emigration, see, for example, Jonathan D. Sarna, *American Judaism: A History*, Yale University Press, 2004, 66. Sarna notes that the waves of Jewish emigration reached a peak in the middle of the nineteenth century, similar to other groups—thus, their emigration was seemingly not an escape from antisemitism. On the other hand, Sarna himself writes that Jewish emigration was "in part a response to the failed liberal revolutions of 1848, and in part a response to the anti-Semitism that came in their wake."
261 "The yearning for a country that would grant genuine equality to them, and to their children after them, was a key element in creating a positive attitude

towards the State of Israel, and it had a metaphysical effect on creating a positive atmosphere towards emigration to Israel," wrote Esther Meir-Glitzenstein in an article, "The Riddle of Mass Aliyah from Iraq," *Pe'amim* 71, 1997, 25–54 [Hebrew].

262 First and foremost, Israel's policies inflame Muslims worldwide. But they also contribute to the spread of antisemitic, or borderline antisemitic, incidents by non-Muslims who oppose Israel's policies in the Middle East and, in particular, its treatment of the Palestinians. For instance, on university campuses where there is intense political activity against Israel, Jewish students report increased harassment, which they view as antisemitism. See: Gil Troy, *The Essential Guide to October 7th and its Aftermath*, JPPI, 2024.

263 See: Shmuel Ettinger, *Contemporary Jewish History*, Dvir, 1969, 276 [Hebrew]. A more widely known opposition to Zionism was voiced by another Jew, Edwin Montagu, who served as Minister of Munitions in the British government and was a cousin of the High Commissioner, Herbert Samuel. Montagu argued that "the demand for recognition as a separate nation put at risk their struggle to become citizens with equal rights in the countries in which they lived." In: Tom Segev, *One Palestine, Complete: Jews and Arabs Under the British Mandate*, Little, Brown, 2000.

264 See: Charles S. Liebman, "Diaspora Influence on Israel: The Ben-Gurion-Blaustein 'Exchange' and its Aftermath," *Jewish Social Studies* 36 (July-October 1974), 271–280. Liebman writes that "the AJC feared that a Jewish state would lead to charges of dual loyalty against Jews and would heighten anti-Semitism."

265 The quote is from: Jerold S. Auerbach, "American Home or Jewish Homeland: The Ben Gurion-Blaustein Debate Reconsidered," *Forum* 40, 58–64.

266 See: Benny Morris, *1948: A History of the First Arab-Israeli War*, Yale University Press, 2008, and Martin Gilbert, *In Ishmael's House: A History of Jews in Muslim Lands*, Yale University Press, 2010.

267 For more on the subject, see: Rosner, *Shtetl, Bagel, Baseball*, 213, ff.

268 See: Rosner and Gil, Jewish and Democratic: Perspectives from World Jewry, 65.

269 And it's worth noting that some predicted this outcome—for example, Hannah Arendt, who wrote: "The anti-Semitism of tomorrow will assert that Jews not only profiteered from the presence of the foreign big powers in the [Middle East] region, but actually plotted it." The quote is from: Leon Wieseltier, "Pariahs and Politics," *New Republic* October 14, 1981.

270 See: Isaiah Berlin, The Crooked Timber of Humanity: Chapters in the History of Ideas, Princeton University Press, 1990, 246.

271 The quote is from the French Jewish thinker, Alain Finkielkraut, *Au nom de l'Autre: Reflexions sur l'antisemitisme qui vient*. Paris: Gallimard, 2003.

272 It refers to Prime Minister Menachem Begin. See: Robert S. Wistrich, *A Lethal Obsession: Anti-Semitism from Antiquity to the Global Jihad*, Random House, 2010, 494.

273 For data about antisemitism in America, see: "Antisemitism in the US," Center for Antisemitism Research, Antidefamation League, 2024.

274 Foer's article was published in The Atlantic, March 2024.

275 Philip Roth, "Some New Jewish Stereotypes," in *Reading Myself and Others*, Farrar Straus and Giroux, 1975, 138.

276 See; Rosner, *Shtetl, Bagel, Baseball.* 46 ff.

277 The quote is from Nirenberg, op cit. Nirenberg is referring to Martin Luther's attacks on the Jews, but his explanation can also be applied to many other examples of attacks on Jews and on Judaism that appear in his book.

278 Data for 2015. See: http://global100.adl.org/. It's worth holding a separate discussion about how Jews were perceived in the great civilizations of Asia, China and India. The fact that Jews living there were not harassed underscores the importance of the religious (mostly Christian) element in the persecution of Jews. For more see: Shalom Salomon Wald, *China and the Jewish People: Old Civilizations in a New Era*, JPPI, 2004.

279 Whether such attitudes are an actual indication of hostility towards Jews is, of course, a question that can be debated. The very measurement of "anti-Semitic attitudes" in this day and age is a complicated undertaking. For example: in 2013, Pew found that 87 percent of Europe's population held a favorable opinion of Jews. On the other hand, a survey conducted by the Anti-Defamation League in 2014 found that negative sentiments about Jews in Western Europe were at an all-time high—24 percent. According to a report published by JPPI, "public opinion polls examining attitudes toward Jews have shown, time and again, contradictory findings." See: *Annual Assessment 2014–2015.* JPPI, 2015, 96.

280 See: *Muslim-Western Tensions Persist.* Global Attitudes Project. Pew, July 2011.

281 See, for example: Jewish People's Experiences and Perceptions of Antisemitism—EU Survey of Jewish People, EU Agency for Fundamental Rights, 2024.

282 See: "Antisemitism on the Rise Down Under," *Tablet Magazine,* July 2024. And see: "The Explosion of Jew-Hate in Trudeau's Canada," *The Free Press*, November 2024.

283 Wistrich, 600.

284 Mark Twain, "Concerning the Jews," *Harper's Magazine*, September 1899.

285 Mark Twain, "Stirring Times in Austria," *Harper's Magazine,* March 1898.

286 The article starts with a reference to a letter Twain received from a lawyer who read his previous article. According to Twain, that letter is what prompted him to write the "sequel." The full text of Twain's article can be read online: https://archive.org/details/concerningthejew014108mbp.

287 See: Dan Vogel, *Mark Twain's Jews*, Ktav Publishing House, 2006, 54 ff. Twain and Herzl first met in Paris, and later on in Vienna as well. Both of them had been deeply affected by the trial of Alfred Dreyfus, the French Jewish officer who was wrongfully accused of treason.

288 For a comprehensive review of such theories and what can be learned from them about the situation of the Jewish people, see Wald, *Rise and Decline of Civilizations: Lessons for the Jewish People*, op cit. Wald offers a list of twelve "drivers" that affect the rise and decline of civilizations: religion, internal solidarity, education and science, language, demography, leadership and the impact of the elites, economic foundations, military ability and the willingness to go to war, diplomatic ties, internal conflict management, chance events ("fortune"), and disasters.

289 Max I. Dimont, *Jews, God and History*, New American Library, 1962. Dimont was interviewed in 1968 by Ofra Elyagon, who in her article mentions that "a million copies of this precious book sold like fresh rolls." According to Wikipedia (without citing any sources), the book has sold over 1.5 million copies.

290 The quotes are from the book itself.

291 Max I. Dimont, *The Indestructible Jews*, The World Publishing, 1971.

292 Dimont chose an interesting model for his book: Lurianic Kabbalah. It talks about the "contraction" of divinity, the "breaking of the vessels" which is articulated, among other things, in the dispersion of Jews among other peoples, and "restoration" which is the aspiration for redemption in the future. In Dimont's book, these three stages are divided into three periods, each lasting 2,000 years. For comparative purposes, refer to the Babylonian Talmud, *Sanhedrin* 97a: "The Tanna Devei Eliyahu teaches that the world is to exist six thousand years: the first two thousand are of confusion, the next two thousand years are of the Torah, and the last two thousand years are the days of the Messiah."

293 The full quote from *Jews, God and History:* "We shall offer for those who cannot accept the theory of a guiding divinity, an explanation for Jewish survival consistent with natural law, never forgetting, however, that throughout this colorful panoply of events and ideas there runs a constant thread—the illusion or dream or revelation of Abraham that the Jews are God's Chosen People."

294 In an article dealing with the "illusion of control," the psychologist Ellen Langer demonstrated the difficulty people have in understanding the role that chance plays in shaping reality. Humans seem to have a powerful need to provide an explanation for phenomena that extends beyond chance, even when it's not necessary. See: Ellen Langer, "The Illusion of Control," *Journal of Personality and Social Psychology* 32(2), August 1975.

295 See Wald, *Rise and Decline of Civilizations: Lessons for the Jewish People*, 414 ff.—"'Fortune' or Chance Events." Wald does not deal with the assumption that survival itself is entirely the result of chance, but rather talks about the dramatic role that chance events played in Jewish history. However, it's clear that if one assumes pivotal events were merely a matter of chance, then the probability of their fortunate sustainability (survival) is also a result of chance.

296 Yovel, New Jewish Time: Jewish Culture in a Secular Age, introduction.

297 Dr. Micah Goodman, who read some of the chapters of my book prior to its publication, commented that the two categories of explanations for the enigma of Jewish survival—God and circumstances—do not necessarily cancel each other out. In the Bible, nearly every occurrence has a dual explanation—one divine and the other human—and they coexist. Why did Joseph go down to Egypt? He went there because of God to fulfill the Covenant Between the Parts, and also because of his brothers who despised him. Is it also possible to live with a contemporary explanation for Jewish survival that contains both types of narratives?

298 The story can be found on the Internet also in the form of an exchange between Louis XIV of France and the philosopher Blaise Pascal. Furthermore, the spirit of the story is consistent with other things Pascal wrote, such as, "For whereas the people of Greece and Italy, of Sparta, Athens and Rome, who came so much later have long since perished, these [the Jews] ever remain, and in spite of the endeavors of many powerful kings who have a hundred times tried to destroy them."

299 Paula Fredriksen, *Augustine and the Jews: A Christian Defense of Jews and Judaism*, Doubleday, 2008. Fredriksen and others are divided over whether Augustine had a favorable view of the Jews, or whether it was a hostile one that just had a tolerable conclusion (because, unlike others, Augustine believed the Jews should be allowed to continue to exist). For a concise summary of the differences of opinion, see, for example, the criticism of Fredriksen's book written by Kevin J. Madigan in *Commentary Magazine* on November 1, 2008.

300 For more about the subject, see: Rosner, *Shtetl, Bagel, Baseball*, 140, ff., in the chapter entitled, "Jesus Loves You." When the 2011 Pew survey asked Evangelicals if the covenant with the Jewish people still exists today, 73 percent answered in the affirmative.

301 The quote is from Shalom Ratzabi, "Religious Thinkers on the Secular State," *Iyunim Bitkumat Israel*, 11 (2001): 1–24 [Hebrew].

302 Jonathan Garb, "Rabbi Kook and His Sources: From Kabbalistic Historiosophy to National Mysticism," in *Studies in Modern Religions, Religious Movements and the Babi-Baha'i Faiths*, ed. Moshe Sharon, Brill, 2004, 77–96.

303 See: Aviezer Ravitzky, *Messianism, Zionism and Jewish Religious Radicalism*. Am Oved, 1993, 156–157 [Hebrew].

304 For further reading, see, for example, David Novak, *Covenantal Rights: A Study in Jewish Political Theory*, Princeton University Press, 2000, 102.

305 *Berakhot,* 32a. This page in the Talmud employs various methods to convey what Moses said in his argument with God. Novak relies on the Rabbi Eleazar's method to illustrate why God is unable to go back on his promise, because there is no force above God that can release Him from it. Therefore, "God cannot annul that oath without destroying his own moral authority."

306 Eliezer Berkovits was one the most prominent Jewish thinkers and rabbis in the United States before moving to Israel. He was born in Romania in 1908 and studied at the Rabbinical Seminary in Berlin, where he served as a rabbi. He escaped from Germany right before the outbreak of World War II, and lived in Australia and the United States, where he also served as a rabbi. In 1975, he relocated to Israel, and died in Jerusalem in 1992.

307 The main points of Berkovits's views on this subject appear in the book: Eliezer Berkovits, *God, Man and History*. Jonathan David, 1959.

308 Edward Gibbon (1737–1794) was an Englishman who wrote the acclaimed book *The History of the Decline and Fall of the Roman Empire.* Francis Fukuyama is an American (1952–) who is mostly known for his bestseller *The End of History and the Last Man.* However, two of his later books are more pertinent to the lessons that this book discusses: *The Origins of Political Order* (2011) and *Political Order and Political Decay: From the Industrial Revolution to the Globalization of Democracy* (2014).

309 Wald briefly compares the endogenous and the exogenous circumstances and reflects on some of the firm conclusions reached by historians who examine a world whose history is "written by the winners, and not the losers."

310 For more about the conversion of Jews under the Christian regime in Spain in the fourteenth century, see: Edward Peters, "Jewish History and Gentile Memory: The Expulsion of 1492," *Jewish History* 9 (Spring 1995): 9–34.

311 Yirmiyahu Yovel, *The Other Within: The Marranos: Split Identity and Emerging Modernity*, Princeton University Press, 2009. Benzion Netanyahu's research maintains that the Marranos did in fact convert to Christianity, and only a small minority of them practiced their Judaism in secret. For more, see: Benzion Netanyahu, *The Marranos of Spain: From the Late 14th Century to the Early 16th Century, According to Contemporary Hebrew Sources*, Cornell University Press, 1999.

312 See: William Horbury, *Jewish War Under Trajan and Hadrian*, Cambridge University Press, 2014; and Jacob Neusner, *A History of the Jews in Babylonia I: The Parthian Period*, Scholars Press, 1969.

313 There is no doubt that Hitler's plan was to annihilate the entire Jewish people, and not just the Jews in Europe. For more about why Hitler wanted to leave no trace of the Jews, see: Snyder, op cit.

314 Michah Goodman phrased it this way: "How do the Jewish people manage to survive? Thanks to biblical promises, according to which the Jews are destined to be the rulers, and the Gentiles, the ruled." See: Michah Goodman, "For the Sake of Remembering You Were Weak," *Makor Rishon*, 2015 [Hebrew].

315 Heinrich Graetz, *History of the Jews vol. I.* 1891.

316 Gidi Grinstein provides an exhaustive description of the balance between "rigidity" and "flexibility" and even merges the two together to form the word "flexigidity" to present his arguments. See: Gidi Grinstein, *Flexigidity: The Secret*

of Jewish Adaptability, self-published, 2013. But it's worth recalling that there were quite a few cases in Jewish history where Jews displayed inflexibility or shed their pragmatic inclinations, leading to tragic outcomes (the days of Bar Kokhba and the rise of Nazism and the Holocaust).

317 Shmuel Safrai, "The Era of the Mishnah and Talmud," in *A History of the Jewish People*, ed. Haim Hillel Ben-Sasson, Harvard University Press, 1976, 307–384.

318 In his book *The Indestructible Jews,* Max Dimont rightly highlights the narrative of the Jews who decided to remain in Babylonia under Persian rule and not return to the Land of Israel during the days of Ezra and until the destruction of the Second Temple. Those Jews were willing exiles, and even though in that period they played only a supporting role in the Jewish drama, one can see them "waiting in the wings, ready to claim the symbolic scepter of Jewish history in the second act."

319 Gadi Taub, *What is Zionism,* Miskal—Yedioth Ahronoth Books and Chemed Books, 2010 [Hebrew].

320 The nature of the *prosbul* regulation and the motivations for enacting it have been the subject of much discussion both in the rabbinical world and among academic researchers, whose understanding of it differs. The historian Salo Baron wrote that "Hillel and members of his generation abolished an explicit law of the Torah." But rabbis who have tried to explain the regulation insist that is not the case. For more about the *prosbul,* see: Dalia Hoshen, "The *Prosbul:* Between Legal Fiction and Jewish Law Drama," *Akdamot* 15 [Hebrew]; and David Bigman, "A Legal Problem or Social Correction? About the Significance of the *Prosbul,"* *Akdamot* 20 [Hebrew].

321 In the early days of Judaism, there is an explicit demand to abstain from writing down the Oral Law. For example in *Tractate Temura* (14b): "He who writes down *halakhot* (laws) is as one who commits the Torah to flames, and whoever studies these written collections has no reward."

322 Certain analyses of the modern-day crisis that Judaism is facing attribute critical significance to the accelerated abolishment of autonomous Jewish communal institutions, and consider that process the impetus for the crisis. As soon as those institutions could no longer impose their will on the Jews, their ability to prevent assimilation was quickly compromised.

323 In this context, it's important to stress that both events were not a matter of cause and effect. The pogroms were an added impetus for migration, whose primary motivations were economic. The catastrophe of the Holocaust enabled the Zionist movement to enlist global support for establishing a Jewish state, but it was not the reason for Israel's founding. Claims that the Holocaust was the main cause of the establishment of the State of Israel are voiced mostly by those who seek to undermine the legitimacy of the Jewish State. For more about Jewish migration, see: Jonathan Sarna, "The Myth of No Return: Jewish

Return Migration to Eastern Europe, 1881–1914," *American Jewish History* 71 (December 1981), 256–268.

324 This is, of course, a highly simplistic and partial depiction of the historical events experienced by the Jews of Spain leading up to their expulsion. However, the expelled Jews without a doubt fueled the growth of the various communities and places they settled in, including Antwerp, Amsterdam, Italy, Greece, Turkey, North Africa, and Safed. For more about the subject, see: Haim Hillel Ben Sasson, *The History of the Jewish People in the Middle Ages*. Dvir, 1969 [Hebrew].

325 Spinoza's treatise was published in 1670.

326 For more about Spinoza and the Jews, see: Robert M. Silverman, *Baruch Spinoza: Outcast Jew, Universal Sage*, Symposium Press, 1995. To understand how the Jews perceived Spinoza and appropriated his theories to meet different needs, starting in Amsterdam in the seventeenth century and up to the present, see: Daniel B. Schwartz, *The First Modern Jew*, Princeton University Press, 2012.

327 The quote is from Yovel, New Jewish Time: Jewish Culture in a Secular Age, introduction.

328 See: Yaakov Geller, "The Jews of India," in *Jews and Judaism in India—Past and Present*, ed. Aryeh Strikovski. Circular on Jewish Culture 271 (2008), Israel Ministry of Education [Hebrew].

329 The quote is from Theological-Political Treatise, 1670.

330 Gidi Grinstein offers this example and expands on it in his book *Flexigidity.* Among other things, he wishes to infer from it that, even today, there is justifiable logic in clinging to the format of a *minyan* of men—as opposed to a mixed one of men and women. Counting both genders in the same *minyan* will decrease by 50 percent the minimum community required for conducting a service. See: Grinstein, 103.

331 Numerous research studies have shown that families with only one Jewish parent have a marked tendency to maintain weaker ties with the Jewish community, observe Jewish rituals less intensively, and attach less importance to the "Jewishness" of the family members. See, for example: Pew, *A Portrait of Jewish Americans.* 2013 (which deals with the largest Jewish community in the world—the one in the United States); and also: Wertheimer and Cohen, op cit.

332 The Babylonian Talmud, *Tractate Eruvin,* 13, says: "For three years there was a dispute between the House of Shammai and the House of Hillel. One said: the *halakha* (law) follows our opinions. And the other said: the *halakha* follows our opinions. And a voice from heaven was heard: These and these are the words of the living God, but the *halakha* follows the House of Hillel. And since these and these are the words of the living God, what entitled the House of Hillel to have the *halakha* fixed according to them? It is because they were lenient and humble, they studied their own opinions and those of the House of Shammai, and even quoted the opinions of the House of Shammai before theirs."

333 Yehuda Bauer is an Israeli historian who was primarily engaged in Holocaust research. The quote is from an interview he gave on the occasion of the publication of his book on Jewish history and its metamorphoses: Yehuda Bauer, *The Impossible People*, Nahar Books, 2013 [Hebrew].

334 The full excerpt from the speech: "As a result of the historic catastrophe in which Titus of Rome destroyed Jerusalem and Israel was exiled from its land, I was born in one of the cities of the Exile. But always I regarded myself as one who was born in Jerusalem. In a dream, in a vision of the night, I saw myself standing with my brother-Levites in the Holy Temple, singing with them the songs of David, King of Israel, melodies such as no ear has heard since the day our city was destroyed and its people went into exile. I suspect that the angels in charge of the Shrine of Music, fearful lest I sing in wakefulness what I had sung in dream, made me forget by day what I had sung at night; for if my brethren, the sons of my people, were to hear, they would be unable to bear their grief over the happiness they have lost. To console me for having prevented me from singing with my mouth, they enable me to compose songs in writing."

335 See: Sacha Stern, Calendar and Community: A History of the Jewish Calendar, 2nd Century BCE—Tenth Century CE, Oxford University Press, 2001, 265.

336 It's interesting to note that version of the Haggadah that is most commonly used today was completed roughly in the same period and first appeared in Rabbi Saadia Gaon's prayer book. See: Shmuel Safrai and Ze'ev Safrai, *Haggadah of the Sages*, Carta, 2007.

337 Gabi Sheffer and Eyal Tsur, For the Sake of Zion I Shall Not Stand Still?: The Jewish Diaspora and the Jerusalem Issue, The Jerusalem Institute for Israel Studies, 2011.

338 See: "Aharon Ben Meir," in Talmudic Encyclopedia, vol. I [Hebrew]; and Moshe Gil, *A History of Palestine, 634–1099*, Cambridge University Press, 1992.

339 For a detailed explanation, see for example, Rahamim Sar Shalom, "The Controversy of R. Saadia and Ben Meir: The Controversy Between Bavel and the Land of Israel Regarding the Principle of the Mean Conjunctions, *Sinai* (1993), 97–124 [Hebrew]. The Talmud contains a number of stories about the authority to decide the number of days in each month, including one that concerns Rabbi Akiva, who would intercalate months outside the Land of Israel because "he did not leave anyone his equal in the Land of Israel." For more about this subject, see the chapter dealing with Babylonia and the Land of Israel in: Sara Zfatman, *From Talmudic Times to the Middle Ages: The Establishment of Leadership in Jewish Literature*, Magnes Press, 2010 [Hebrew].

340 Sacha Stern, 267.

341 Regarding this matter, see, for example, Danzig's discussion about the epistles written by the Babylonian, Pirqoi ben Baboi, in Neil Danzig, "New Leaves from Pirqoi ben Baboi, in *Shalem* Vol. 8, ed. Joseph R. Hacker, Ben Zvi Institute, 2008, 2 [Hebrew]. "According to Rabbi Pirqoi, the law in the Land of Israel

was fundamentally flawed due to the *shmad* (restrictions forbidding Jews from practicing Judaism]) that halted the living tradition of the Oral Law in the Land of Israel, as opposed to the living and uninterrupted tradition of Babylonian Talmudic law."

342 See: Menahem Ben Sasson, "Varieties of Inter-Communal Relations in the Geonic Period," in *The Jews of Medieval Islam: Community, Society and Identity*, Brill, 1995, 19.

343 For the full text of the Proclamation of Independence: http://www.knesset.gov.il/docs/eng/megilat_eng.htm.

344 As opposed to many other peoples who seek to highlight the indigenous elements of their national narrative and present it as a story of the original settlers of their country, the Jewish people is fixed on a narrative according to which they are not the native population of what would later become their homeland. See: Moshe Greenberg, *On the Bible and Judaism: A Collection of Writings*, Am Oved, 1984 [Hebrew].

345 See: Franz Rosenzweig, *Naharayim: A Selection of Writings*. Bialik Institute, 1977 [Hebrew].

346 In his famous commentary on the first verse of the Book of Genesis, Rashi (Rabbi Shlomo Yitzchaki) identifies this right commencing with the decision to start the Torah with the story of Creation. For more about Rashi's choice of that commentary and its historical circumstances, see: Elazar Touitou, "The Historical Background of Rashi's Commentary on the Bereshit Torah Portion," in *Rashi Studies*, Bar-Ilan University Press, 1993, 97–105 [Hebrew].

347 In the Bible, the Land of Israel is called the Land of Canaan, named after its inhabitants who lived there before the Israelites. "The Bible rejects the notion of an organic, unmediated connection between a people and its land. Still, it does not take issue with the basic idea of territory; instead, it offers a unique doctrine, one which anchors the Hebrews' territorial rights to the Land of Israel in a decree by the supreme divine authority—and in that alone." Assaf Sagiv, "Zionism and the Myth of Motherland," *Azure*, Autumn 1998.

348 In 2015, around 43 percent of all Jews worldwide (14.2 million) lived in Israel. See the Demography chapter in: *Annual Assessment 2014–2015*. JPPI, 2015.

349 For a discussion about this issue, see: Eliezer Schweid, *Homeland and a Land of Promise*, Am Oved, 1979 [Hebrew]. As Schweid notes, "there is no doubt whatsoever that the Jews existed as a people out of an awareness of their bond with the Land of Israel, and there is no doubt whatsoever that the peoples among whom the Jews lived, and who also alternately ruled their land, acknowledged the connection between the Jews and their land."

350 Regarding the significance of the establishment of the State of Israel for "the nature of Judaism itself," see: *Akdamot* 30, 15 [Hebrew]. "In practice, the establishment of the State of Israel was the deciding factor in the historical debate about messianism in Judaism."

351 In recent decades, some researchers have added important insights which either refute or temper the claim that the Jews were powerless during their long years of exile. See: David Biale, *Power and Powerlessness in Jewish History*, Schocken Books, 1986.

352 This depiction is a paraphrase of Moshe Halbertal, "Modern Jewish Identities and the State of Israel," op cit.

353 It should be stressed that Koestler's conclusion stems, among other things, from his notion of Judaism as a religion. He even notes that it won't be difficult for assimilated Jews to preserve the values of Judaism because "its essential teachings have passed long ago into the mainstream of the Judeo-Christian heritage." Arthur Koestler, *Promise and Fulfillment, Palestine 1917–1949*, Macmillan, 1914, 335.

354 For a clear and concise summary of the principles and history of Zionism, see Taub, op cit.

355 For more about Dubnow's point of view, see: Robert Seltzer, Simon Dubnow's 'New Judaism': Diaspora Nationalism and the World History of the Jews, Brill, 2014.

356 For more about Cohen (1842–1918), see: Eliezer Schweid, *A History of Modern Religious Philosophy, part III vol. I (Vol. 1)*, Am Oved, 2003, 115 [Hebrew]. For Cohen's views, see: Hermann Cohen, *Religion of Reason: Out of the Sources of Judaism*, trans. Simon Kaplan. Frederick Unger, 1972.

357 See, for example: Grinstein, op cit.

358 A lengthy and detailed discussion concerning this matter can be found in Joseph Turner, *The Relation to Zion and the Diaspora in 20th Century Jewish Thought: A Study in the Philosophy of Jewish Existence*, Hakibbutz Hameuchad, 2014 [Hebrew].

359 The loss of faith in the Emancipation also means acknowledging that the attempt to separate an individual's Jewish identity from the national identity of his place of residence contains something artificial. When the country doesn't shut down for Yom Kippur and Jews have to go to work, then their individual identity is also compromised. For more about the subject see: Shlomo Avineri, *Varieties of Zionist Thought*, Am Oved, 1980 [Hebrew].

360 Cohen's philosophy draws a lot from Kant as well as Maimonides. For more about the subject, see: Emil L. Fackenheim, *Hermann Cohen, After Fifty Years*, Leo Baeck Institute, 1969.

361 For more about Cohen's views about Zionism, see Nathan Rotenstreich's introduction to Hermann Cohen, *Studies in Judaism and the Problems of Our Generation: Selected Essays from Judische Schriften*, trans. Zvi Wislawski. Bialik Institute, 1977 [Hebrew]. A detailed description of the dispute between Hermann Cohen and Martin Buber over Zionism can be found in Turner, op cit., and in Joseph Turner, "The Hermann Cohen-Martin Buber Controversy Over Zionism," *Iyunim Bitkumat Israel*, 17 (2007): 155–178 [Hebrew].

362 See: Erich S. Gruen, "the Emergence of the Jewish Diaspora, in *New Jewish Time: Jewish Culture in a Secular Age*, op cit., 196 [Hebrew].

363 Hertzberg and Hirt-Manheimer, op cit.

364 Ben-Zion Dinaburg, ed., *The Book of Zionism*. Bialik Institute and Tel Aviv: Dvir, 1939 [Hebrew].

365 For more about the traits of the new Jew, see: Yitzhak Conforti, "'The New Jew' in the Zionist Movement: Ideology and Historiography," *Australian Journal of Jewish Studies* 25 (2011): 89–121.

366 Sergio DellaPergola, Jewish Demography: Facts, Outlook, Challenges. JPPI, 2003.

367 In Israel, there's no need to choose to be Jewish or make an effort to be Jewish because communal life is Jewish life. For a detailed description of the way Israel reformulated the "Jewishness" of Israelis see: *#IsraeliJudaism, A Portrait of Cultural Revolution*, Shmuel Rosner, Camil Fuchs, JPPI, 2018. In the Diaspora, there is a need to choose and invest in choosing a Jewish life. See: Rosner, *Shtetl, Bagel, Baseball*, chapter 3.

368 Conflicts of this nature were particularly prominent in 2015, the year this book was written: whether against the backdrop of the confrontation between the Israeli government and the US administration under President Barack Obama (concerning Iran's nuclear capability and the Israeli-Palestinian peace process); or against the backdrop of the outbreak of antisemitism in Europe, and especially in France, followed by the appeal to French Jews to move to Israel); or against the backdrop of the opposing views between most Jews worldwide and the Jews living in Israel, which were evident in the Israeli elections held at the beginning of 2015. For more about that subject, see the "Bonds Between Communities" chapter in the JPPI's Annual Assessment 2014–2015. Similar confrontations emerged in other periods, as well.

369 For further reading, see: Rosner, *Shtetl, Bagel, Baseball*, chapter 7, and: Caryn Aviv and David Shneer, *New Jews: The End of the Jewish Diaspora*, NYU Press, 2005.

370 Despite the much larger scope of the issue, it's worth making at least brief mention of the fact that Zionism abandoned *de facto,* if not *de jure,* the definition of Judaism as primarily a religion, and adopted the definition of Judaism as primarily a nationality, See Taub, op cit., 35. "The state that Zionism created is based on a secular definition of identity in its constitutional framework, and it's certainly not the state of the Jewish religion. It's the state of the Jewish nationality."

371 A fascinating discussion about Nachmanides's worldview and the religious controversy over the question of fulfilling the Commandments outside the Land of Israel can be found in "Set Yourself Signs," one of the essays appearing in: Aviezer Ravitzky, *Al Daat Hamakom: Essays in the History of Jewish Philosophy*, Keter, 1991, 34–71 [Hebrew].

372 Nachmanides's worldview relies on Sifre on Deuteronomy: "Although I may exile you from the Land, you must excel in the fulfillment of the commandments, so that when you return to the Land, they will not be new to you." Ravitzky, op cit.

373 The matter of the 'earth of the Land of Israel'—namely, whether one can and should establish a Jewish political entity that is of value only in the Land of Israel—was on the agenda in certain early periods of political Zionism awakening. In his wide-ranging and engaging book, Adam Rovner describes the evolvement of the ideas to settle the Jews in New York, East Africa (what is known as the Uganda Plan), Angola, Madagascar, Tasmania, and Suriname. See: Adam Rovner, *In the Shadow of Zion: Promised Lands Before Zion*, NYU Press, 2014.

374 The quote appears in: A. B. Yehoshua, "Defining Who is an Israeli," *Haaretz*, September 12, 2013 [Hebrew].

375 The quote appears in Conforti, op. cit.

376 See: The A.B. Yehoshua Controversy: An Israel-Diaspora Dialogue on Jewishness, Israeliness, and Identity. American Jewish Committee, 2006.

377 See for example: Shmuel Rosner, "Is There a Way to Defend A. B. Yehoshua's Miserable Display?," *Jewish Journal*, June 2, 2014, and Rosner, *Shtetl, Bagel, Baseball*, 301.

378 For more about their views, see Turner, The Relation to Zion and the Diaspora in the 20th Century, 270.

379 Daniel Boyarin, *A Radical Jew: Paul and the Politics of Identity*, University of California Press, 1997.

380 The claim in recent years has been that young Jews, especially in the United States, are less inclined to support Zionism. That claim is the subject of a bitter debate among thinkers and researchers. Either way, it's clear that the Jews' perception of Zionism has changed over the years. For further reading, see: Theodore Sasson, *The New American Zionism*, NYU Press, 2013.

381 The Jewish American historian Jonathan Sarna, made a distinction between "European Zionism" where Diaspora-negation was prevalent, and "American Zionists who tended to dismiss it out of hand." See: Jonathan D. Sarna, "The Question of *Shlilat HaGalut* in American Zionism," in *Beyond Survival and Philanthropy: American Jewry and Israel*, eds. Allon Gal and Alfred Gottschalk. Hebrew Union College Press, 2000.

382 For more about Kaplan and his worldview, see: Mel Scult, *The Radical American Judaism of Mordecai M. Kaplan*, Indiana University Press, 2013. And also: Nicham Ross, "Jewish Identity without Judaism in the Thought of Ahad Ha-am and Mordecai Kaplan," *International Journal of Jewish Education Research* 5–6 (2013): 23–51 [Hebrew].

383 Mordecai M. Kaplan, *A New Zionism*, Herzl Press and the Jewish Reconstructionist Press, 1959. Kaplan revised his views on Zionism following the establishment of the State of Israel and due to a certain disappointment

with its character. He also believed that the "reconstruction of Jewish life in the Diaspora was a condition for repairing the Land of Israel." See: Turner, *The Relation to Zion and the Diaspora in the 20th Century*, 178 ff.

384 For more about Abba Hillel Silver's Zionism, see: Mark A. Raider, Jonathan D. Sarna and Ronald W. Zweig, eds. *Abba Hillel Silver and American Zionism*, Frank Cass Publishers, 1977.

385 For more about Silver's life and work, see: Marc Lee Raphael. *Abba Hillel Silver: A Profile in American Judaism*, Lynne Rienner Publishers, 1989.

386 An interesting discussion about Silver's and Ben-Gurion's different leadership styles can be found in: Anita Shapira, "Silver and Ben-Gurion: Two Types of Leadership," in Raider, Sarna and Zweig, 33–44.

387 For a description of that struggle, see: Ofer Shiff, *The Downfall of Abba Hillel Silver and the Foundation of Israel*, Syracuse University Press, 2014.

388 The quote is from Ofer Shiff, "Abba Hillel Silver and the Perception of the New Diaspora Jew Following the Establishment of the State of Israel," *Israel* 16 (2009), 227–249 [Hebrew].

389 Quoted in Shiff, Ibid, 233.

390 See: Shmuel Rosner, "Israel Gave Up on the Negation of the Diaspora," *Jewish Journal*, December 2011.

391 For more about the evolvement of Judah Halevi's worldview, see: Micah Goodman, *The Dream of the Kuzari*. Dvir, 2012, 198–205 [Hebrew].

392 There is a lack of consensus over whether Halevi actually reached the shores of the Land of Israel, or died prior to that. See: S. D. Goitein, "Did Yehuda Halevi Arrive in the Land of Israel," *Tarbiz* 46 (Autumn 1977), 245, [Hebrew].

393 For more about the subject, see: Ben-Zion Dinur, "Rabbi Judah Halevi's Immigration to the Land of Israel and the Messianic Ferment in His Time, in Ben-Zion Dinur, *Historical* Writings, Bialik Institute, 1975 [Hebrew].

394 For poll numbers that prove this claim see for example: Voice of the People Index, JPPI, July 2024.

395 Professor Yossi Shain posits that Jewish identity, overall, has in recent decades undergone "Israelization," which is transforming its nature and essence. See: *The Israeli Century: How the Zionist Revolution Changed History and Reinvented Judaism, Yossi Shain*, Wicked Son, 2021.

396 That was Disraeli's response to an Irish member of Parliament who ridiculed his Jewish origins.

397 The story in its entirety appears in an article written by one of Einstein's biographers, Walter Isaacson, based on a collection of letters that the physicist wrote: Walter Isaacson, "How Einstein Divided America's Jews," *The Atlantic*, October 11, 2009. The Weizmann quote appears in additional sources, including for example: David Bodanis, *Einstein's Greatest Mistake: A Biography*, Houghton Mifflin Harcourt, 2016.

398 Steven Gimbel, Einstein's Jewish Science: Physics at the Intersection of Politics and Religion, Johns Hopkins University Press, 2012.

399 Freud shared Einstein's insight: "You can rest assured that had my name been Uberhuber, my innovations would have met much less opposition," he wrote in 1908 to his student Karl Abraham.

400 See: Voltaire. *Toleration and Other Essays*, trans. Joseph McCabe. G. P. Putnam's Sons, 1912, 251. And: Paul Mendes-Flohr and Jehuda Reinharz, eds. *The Jew in the Modern World: A Documentary History*, Oxford University Press, 1980, 252.

401 The quote is from Jonathan Sacks, *Future Tense: Jews, Judaism and Israel in the Twenty-First Century*, Hodder & Stoughton, 2209, 207. Irving Berlin was a composer, Isaiah Berlin was a philosopher. In his book, Sacks mentions the names of many other Jews who revolutionized the world, ranging from Karl Marx and Karl Popper to Erich Fromm and Jacques Derrida.

402 A wealth of data on this issue can be found in: Charles Murray, "Jewish Genius," *Commentary*, April 1, 2007.

403 In: Steven Pinker, "Groups and Genes: The Lessons of the Ashkenazim," *New Republic*, June 20, 2006.

404 Reasons that explain Israel's excellence in the hi-tech industry can be found in: Dan Senor and Saul Singer, *Start-Up Nation: The Story of Israel's Economic Miracle*, Council on Foreign Relations, 2009. Other books describe Israel's contribution to specific fields, such as the development of technology to address worldwide water shortages. See: Seth M. Siegel, *Let There Be Water: Israel's Solution for a Water-Starved World*, Thomas Dunne Books, 2015.

405 In his book *Outliers,* Malcolm Gladwell devotes a chapter to the success of Jewish lawyers in New York: Malcolm Gladwell, *Outliers: The Story of Success*, Little, Brown, 2008. The success of Jewish investment bankers is the subject of the top selling book by Stephen Birmingham, *Our Crowd: The Great Jewish Families of New York*, Harper and Row, 1967. Although it remained on the bestseller list for quite some time, there were also a number of reservations about the book's value as historical nonfiction. Yet the fact that it was even written, its popularity, and the interest it generated testify to the fact that the Jews' success in New York's financial markets is a story worthy of special attention. Important Jewish financiers also lived in Muslim countries and North Africa. Perhaps the most prominent among them was Yehezkel Sasson, who served as Iraq's minister of finance and laid some of the foundations of modern Iraq.

406 Some have, however, also denied that, such as the historian Cecil Roth, who claimed that "persons of Jewish birth have taken, not indeed a dominant, nor a disproportionate share, but a share worthy of study and respect." See: Cecil Roth, *The Jewish Contribution to Civilisation*, Macmillan, 1938, 364.

407 See, for example, the interesting discussion about biblical texts and narratives that made their way to the Koran: Bat-Sheva Garsiel, *Bible, Midrash and Quran:*

An Intertextual Study of Common Narrative Materials, Hakibbutz Hameuchad, 2006 [Hebrew].

408 For more about the Talmud's surprising influence on perceptions of Jews and Judaism in South Korea, see: Ross Arbes, "How the Talmud Became a Best-Seller in South Korea," *The New Yorker*, June 23, 2015.

409 Flavius Josephus, *Against Apion* Book II, Section 26.

410 See: Maristella Botticini and Zvi Eckstein, "Jewish Occupational Selection: Education, Restrictions, or Minorities?" *Journal of Economic History* 65 (2005), 1–26. Botticini and Eckstein demonstrate quite convincingly that Jews moved into different occupations even before pressures from their non-Jewish surroundings forced them to do so. Their explanation for the change: a comparatively higher literacy rate that began further to reforms in the Jewish world and a transition from performing rites to learning, which in turn led to a slow and gradual process of the Jews' integration in occupations that gave them an inherent advantage. When writing this chapter, I relied in no small degree on Botticini and Eckstein's engaging research. It should, however, be noted that their research has received a fair share of criticism and that other theories about the origins of Jewish literacy also exist. For instance, in his controversial book, the geneticist Cyril Darlington claimed that the surge in the value of literacy actually began after the destruction of the First Temple and the exile of the Jewish elite to Babylonia. The Jews who stayed behind in the Land of Israel were "working class" and began assimilating. Therefore, when they returned from Babylonia to Jerusalem, the exiles, the members of the elite, comprised the majority of the Jewish community. See: Cyril Dean Darlington, *The Evolution of Man and Society*, Allen & Unwin, 1969.

411 The available sources dealing with the Sadducees are sparse and not necessarily accurate as much of the research relies on rabbinical literature—which for the most part is biased. See: Eyal Regev, *The Sadducees and Their Halakhah: Religion and Society in the Second Temple Period*, Ben Zvi Institute, 2005 [Hebrew]. Who these groups were is not entirely clear, and the accepted assertion that the Romans prevailed over the Sadducees and that rabbinical Judaism is an extension of the Pharisees, may not be true.

412 See: Maristella Botticini and Zvi Eckstein, "From Farmers to Merchants, Voluntary Conversions and Diaspora: Human Capital and Jewish History," *Journal of the European Economic Association* 5 (2007), 887. Botticini and Eckstein point out that most of the Jews who converted to Christianity in the beginning of the first millennium came from the uneducated classes, which led to a higher rate of literacy among the Jews who did not.

413 See: Raphael Patai, *The Jewish Mind*, Wayne State University Press, 1977, 317–320. George Sarton's research found that 95 of the world's 626 most outstanding scientists—15 percent—were Jews, although their share of the general population was around one-half of one percent. The figures are even

more impressive with regard to specific countries: in Spain, the Jews constituted 2.7 percent of the population, but 41.2 percent of the scientists; in France, the Jews were less than one percent of the population, but over 25 percent of the scientists; in Germany and Western Europe, they were 0.83 percent of the population, but 21.4 percent of the scientists.

414 Salo Baron took issue with the explanation that attributed considerable importance to the restrictions on land ownership that were imposed on the Jews. The question of the religious authorization to engage in money lending pertains to Jews in Christian areas. Baron believed that the transition to financial occupations also derived from the high degree of literacy that these occupations required.

415 The quote is from: Jacques Attali, *Les Juifs le monde et l'argent*, Paris: Fayard, 2002.

416 Shmuel Ettinger, "The Modern Period," in *A History of the Jewish People*, ed. Haim Hillel Ben-Sasson, 743.

417 The divine providence explanation often comes from surprising places. For instance, Benjamin Disraeli, Britain's Jewish-born Prime Minister who converted to Christianity, believed that Jews had an "exalted racial birthright" and also benefited from "divine protection." See: Michael Makovsky. *Churchill's Promised Land: Zionism and Statecraft,* Yale University Press, 2007, 42.

418 See, for example, the warning of the renowned Harvard University scientist, Steven Pinker, who researched the origins of intelligence among Ashkenazi Jews (see a previous endnote in this chapter). One can only imagine, Pinker writes, what will happen when a research study can indicate that Jews have a natural inclination for success in money lending. Pinker, op cit.

419 See: "New Findings Concerning the Genome Structure of the Jewish People, *Annual Assessment 2010,* Jerusalem: JPPI, 2011, 201–203.

420 See: Michael F. Hammer, et al. "Y Chromosomes of Jewish Priests," *Nature*, 385 (1997).

421 As noted, the study's powerful political connotations and the criticism it generated cannot be ignored. See, for instance, Nadia Abu El-Haj's controversial book: Nadia Abu El-Haj, *The Genealogical Science: The Search for Jewish Origins and the Politics of Epistemology*, University of Chicago Press, 2012. On page 37, she refers to the research concerning the Jewish priests as a piece in a puzzle whose aim is to frame a historical identity for the Jewish people.

422 Susan M. Adams, et al. "The Genetic Legacy of Religious Diversity and Intolerance: Paternal Lineages of Christians, Jews and Muslims in the Iberian Peninsula," *American Journal of Human Genetics* 83 (2008), 725–736. And: Gil Atzmon, et al. "Abraham's Children in the Genome Era: Major Jewish Diaspora Populations Comprise Distinct Genetic Clusters with Shared Middle Eastern Ancestry," *American Journal of Human Genetics* 86 (2010), 850–859. See also a book published by one the researchers of the latter article: Harry Ostrer, *Legacy: A Genetic History of the Jewish People*, Oxford University Press, 2012.

As a few critics have noted, Ostrer digresses from purely scientific writing and makes some sweeping and clearly controversial statements, such as his assertion at the beginning of the book that "in June 2010, I published a scientific article that demonstrated a biological basis for Jewishness"—or his attempt to vindicate Zionist claims using DNA. See: Paul S. Appelbaum and Diana Muir Appelbaum, "A Problematic Reading of the Genetic History of the Jews," *GeneWatch* 27 (May-July 2014), which is available online on the Council for Responsible Genetics website, and: Richard C. Lewontin, "Is There a Jewish Gene?" *The New York Review of Books*, December 6, 2012.

423 For a professional-academic critique of that theory, see: R. Brian Ferguson, *How Jews Became Smart: Anti-"Natural History of Ashkenazi Intelligence,"* January 2008. This article is published through ResearchGate. https://www.ncas.rutgers.edu/sites/fasn/files/How%20Jews%20Became%20Smart%20(2008).pdf

424 See, for example, a rather delayed response to this research, which created a lot of buzz because, among other things, the researcher is an Israeli: Eran Elhaik, "The Missing Link of Jewish European Ancestry: Contrasting the Rhineland and the Khazarian Hypotheses," *Genome Biology and Evolution* 5 (2013), 61–74. It is Elhaik's claim that Ashkenazi Jews are descended from the Khazars.

425 See: Noah J. Efron, *Judaism and Science: A Historical Introduction*. Greenwood Press, 200, 3.

426 See Editor's Note attached to Bret Stephens, "The Secrets of Jewish Genius," *The New York Times,* December 2019.

427 See: Gregory Cochran, Jason Hardy and Henry Harpending, "Natural History of Ashkenazi Intelligence, *Journal of Biosocial Science* 38 (September 2006), 659–693. When this paper was published, some dismissed it. Andrew Clark, a population geneticist at Cornell, called its arguments "far-fetched." One of the authors of that study, Harpending, was described as having a "white nationalist" ideology by the Southern Poverty Law Center.

428 This much talked about research deals with Ashkenazi Jews, as do the most of the other genetic studies about Jews. The focus on Ashkenazi Jews can to be attributed to a few factors: firstly, they carry more genetic disorders that are the subject of medical research; secondly, they are the largest group of Jews and comprised the vast majority of world Jewry prior to World War II. (See: Sergio DellaPergola, "Some Fundamentals of Jewish Demographic History," in *Papers in Jewish Demography*, eds. Sergio DellaPergola and Judith Even. Hebrew University, 2001, 11–33; thirdly, Ashkenazi Jews are the major Jewish group in the countries where this kind of genetic research has been conducted.

429 See: Richard Lynn, "The Intelligence of American Jews," *Personality and Individual Differences*, 36 (2004), 201–206.

430 See: Jon Entine, Abraham's Children: Race, Identity and the DNA of the Chosen People, Grand Central Publishing, 2007.

431 See: Robert Wistrich, "There's Only One God and We Don't Believe in Him!: About Freud as a Jew," *Haaretz*, 2006 [Hebrew].
432 The quote is from Dubnow, 159.
433 Yuri Slezkine, *The Jewish Century*, Princeton University Press, 2004.
434 See Bodanis, 23 and Michael Eckert, *Arnold Sommerfeld: Science, Life and Turbulent Times 1868–1951*, Springer, 2013. Because Sommerfeld was highly vocal in his defense of Einstein and other Jewish scientists, the Nazis labeled him "an agent of Judaism in German intellectual life" in an article published in the SS magazine in 1937.
435 The historian Paul Johnson believes that from "an intellectual perspective," Einstein belonged to the rationalist tradition "of Maimonides and of Spinoza." Paul Johnson, 418. His insight regarding a "scientific Torah" appears on p. 420.
436 See: Alexander L. Ringer, *Arnold Schoenberg: The Composer as Jew*, Clarendon Press, 1990.
437 See: Robert Blake. *Disraeli*. Eyre & Spottiswoode, 1966 (reprinted by Prion Books, 1988), as well as Makovsky, op cit.
438 See Todd Endelman's review of another biography of Disraeli (cited below): Todd M. Endelman, "The Making of Benjamin Disraeli: Adam Kirsch's New Biography," *The New York Sun*, September 17, 2008.
439 James Hawes attaches little importance to the fact that Kafka was Jewish: James Hawes, *Excavating Kafka*, Quercus, 2008. Sander Gilman, on the other hand, believes it has considerable importance: Sander L. Gilman, *Franz Kafka, the Jewish Patient,* Routledge, 1995.
440 Adam Kirsch's biography of Disraeli was published as part of a series whose protagonists are Jews (Jewish Encounters). Kirsch writes: "Disraeli's Jewishness was the central fact about him, the thing that no one could forget or ignore." See: Adam Kirsch, *Benjamin Disraeli*, Schocken Books, 2008, 19.
441 When asked who was the center of gravity at the 1878 Congress of Berlin, Bismarck pointed to Disraeli—"Der alte Jude." The story appears in: Henry Kissinger, *Diplomacy*, Simon & Schuster, 1994, 155.
442 The discrepancy in the book's title stems, of course, from its target audience. The premise is that the Israeli reader will be much more "interested" in Disraeli the "Jew" than Disraeli the "earl." Cecil Roth, *Disraeli, Earl of Beaconsfield*, Philosophical Library, 1952.
443 Cecil Roth, The Jewish Contribution to Civilisation, op cit.
444 For more about Maimonides's views about the End of Days and the coming of the Messiah, see: Yeshayahu Leibowitz, "Messianic Redemption in Maimonides's Philosophy," in *Faith, History and Values*, op cit. See also: Moses Maimonides, *Epistle to Yemen*, in which Maimonides talks about the image of the Messiah, and, Aviezer Ravitsky, "To the Utmost Capacity: Maimonides on the Days of the Messiah," in Aviezer Ravitsky, *History and Faith: Studies in Jewish Philosophy,* Amsterdam: J.C. Gieben, 1996, 73–112.

445 Alain Elkann, *Mitzva*, Bompiani, 2004 [Italian].

446 See: Shmuel Feiner, *Moses Mendelssohn: Sage of Modernity*. trans. Anthony Berris. Yale University Press, 2010. See also: Alexander Altmann, *Moses Mendelssohn: A Biographical Study*, University of Alabama Press, 1973. One of Mendelssohn's grandsons, the composer Felix Mendelssohn, received some good advice from his converted father: "Drop the name of your famous father because there can no more be a Christian Mendelssohn than there can be a Jewish Confucius."

447 The original quote: "Up to the year 1823, there were no less than 1,236 conversions in Berlin, comprising half of the members of the community." Heinrich Graetz, *History of the Jews vol. V*, 1891.

448 The demographer, Sergio DellaPergola maintains that "throughout the 19th century, there are initial indications of secularization and assimilation processes among the Jews. Those processes led to an estimated contraction of the Jewish community by around 200,000 Jews in the 19th century alone." See: Sergio DellaPergola, "Demography and Jewish Peoplehood," in *Studies of the Jewish People.*

449 Specific documentation pertaining to the assimilation of Berlin's Jews and its underlying reasons can be found in: Deborah Hertz, *How Jews Became Germans: The History of Conversion and Assimilation in Berlin*, Yale University Pres, 2007. Hertz describes the "vulnerability" of Judaism in different periods as well as the tremendous economic and social pressures that led many Jews to opt for conversion.

450 Some could argue that, in certain countries, the utilitarian explanation actually suggests that conversion to Judaism is a rational act, especially in the United States where the Jews enjoy a favorable image and are accepted by the rest of the population (see Putnam and Campbell's research, who found that the Jews are the best-liked religious group in America: Robert D. Putnam and David E. Campbell, *American Grace: How Religion Divides Is and Unites Us*, Simon & Schuster, 2010).

451 From the point of view of Jewish continuity, not all Jews are alike," wrote the researcher, Steven Cohen, when explaining why mixed couples—between a Jew and non-Jew—have less ability to ensure the future of Jewish existence. Granted, a sizeable percentage of those who married non-Jews also say they are "Jewish." But by saying that, some of those Jews are not articulating something which has any practical meaning in their lives. Consequently, their chances of raising another generation of Jews are much lower. See: Steven M. Cohen, "Can Intermarriage Lead to an Increase in the Number of Jews in America?" *Mosaic Magazine*, November 9, 2015. Cohen's article is a link in a long chain of publications that aim to assess how many offspring of mixed couples are likely to remain Jewish. For a different point of view, see: Theodore Sasson, et al., *Millennial Children of Intermarriage: Touchpoints and Trajectories of Jewish Engagement*, op. cit.

452 Obviously, for certain people, assimilation is something significant and desirable—whether they are Israelis who want to sever their Israeliness from the Jewish past that engendered it and redirect it to a future of shared nationalism for "all Israel's citizens" (see the petitions pertaining to this matter which have been filed with the Israeli courts, including the petition filed by Uzzi Ornan, who wanted the word "Israeli" to be entered as his nationality in the Population Registry. Refer to the rulings of the District Court and Supreme Court in the matter of *Ornan et al. v. the Ministry of Interior, et al.* The court rejected the argument made by the petitioners who sought recognition of an Israeli nationality. Justice Noam Solberg wrote that "in legal and judicial terms—there is no such thing as an Israeli nationality," and that "the court must not create something out of nothing")—or whether they are Jews, especially in the Diaspora, who find no interest or benefit in keeping a tradition that is obsolete. They are not ashamed of their Jewish origin, but they also attach little importance to it. Their Jewish origin is a "fact" they recognize, but it doesn't "incur any special sense of belonging or obligation" (the quote is from an article by my JPPI colleague, Dr. Shlomo Fischer about the largest group of Jews who in his recent research are called "Jews of no religion." Shlomo Fischer, "Who are the 'Jews by Religion" in the Pew Report?" *The Time of Israel*, November 18, 2013.

453 See the discussion about Americans of Jewish background in the Pew study *A Portrait of Jewish Americans*, chapter 7: "People of Jewish Background and Jewish Affinity." For an abridged version and easy read, see: Michael Lipka, "How Many Jews are there in the United States?," Pew, October 2, 2013.

454 Nearly all the research studies dealing with Jewish communities around the world identify a Jewish network of friends as an indicator of the strength of one's Jewish identity and the prospects for Jewish continuity. See, for example, the Australian research: Andrew Markus, "Overview," in *Jewish Continuity*, ed. Andrew Markus. Monash University, 2011, or the American research: Cohen, Ukeles and Miller, *Special Study on "Partly Jewish" Jews*, op cit.

455 Leo Strauss delivered his buzz-generating lecture, "Why We Remain Jews," at the University of Chicago in 1964. See Deutsch and Nicgorski, 43.

456 See: Emil L. Fackenheim, *To Mend the World: Foundations of Future Jewish Thought*. Schocken Books, 1982, and also: Eliezer Schweid, "Is There a Religious Meaning to the Idea of a Chosen People after the Shoah?" in *The Impact of the Holocaust on Jewish Theology*, ed. Steven T. Katz. NYU Press, 2005, 5–12.

457 Not everyone will agree with my assertion. Some emphasize the early appearance of the Jewish mission of *tikkun olam* in the writings of the Latter Prophets or even in the Torah (mentioned in a previous note). In my view, their claim and the way they interpret its implications for Judaism in the present are themselves an interpretation of Judaism that incorporates a modern vantage point which is possible, but not imperative. Obviously, this modern understanding of the Jewish mission is not different than any other interpretation of a tradition,

which is made by a person observing it in a particular time and aims to adapt the current reality to past traditions.

458 Krochmal was born in 1785 and died in 1840. More about him can be found in Yehoyada Amir, "The Perplexity of Our Time: Rabbi Nachman Krochmal and Modern Jewish Existence," *Modern Judaism* 23 (October 2009), 264–301, and in Louis Jacobs, *The Book of Jewish Belief*. Behrman House, 1984, 83.

459 The third Hebrew edition of the book is available on the Herzog College website. The edition edited by Yehoyada Amir is easier to understand, but it too is not particularly user-friendly to the contemporary reader: Nachman Krochmal, *Guide of the Perplexed of the* Time, ed. Yehoyada Amir. Carmel, 2011 [Hebrew].

460 Eliezer Schweid, "A Guide of the Perplexed for the Perplexed of Our Time," *Kivunim Hadashim* 26 (June 2012) [Hebrew]. See also: Micah Goodman, "Between the Perplexity of the Time and Studying the History of the Time: A New Look at Rabbi Nachman Krochmal's Philosophy," *Daat* 57–59 [Hebrew]. It's also worth reading Schlomo Weissblueth's short article about the concept of redemption in Krochmal's thinking who writes: "Redemption is a transitional state in Israel's history, between period and period, from one level to a higher level, primarily from a spiritual perspective. These states are recurring acts and are an expression of the nation's perpetuity." Schlomo Weissblueth, "Exile and Redemption in Rabbi Nachman Krochmal's Philosophy," in *Redemption and State—The Redemption of Israel, Vision and Reality: People and State According to Judaism*, 121–128 [Hebrew].

461 For more about Krochmal's ideas, see: Jay M. Harris, *Nachman Krochmal: Guiding the Perplexed of the Modern Time*, NYU Press, 1991, and, in particular chapter 3, which deals with Krochmal's historical theory.

462 Harris, 128.

463 The origin of a light unto the nations is a verse in the Book of Isaiah: "I, the Lord, have called you in righteousness; and have taken hold of your hand and I formed you, and I made you to be a covenant for the people, a light to nations." (Isaiah 42:6). *Tikkun olam* comes from the expression "perfect the world under the Kingdom of God," which appears in the *Aleinu LeShabeach* prayer (which was originally written for the kingdom prayer on Rosh Hashana). The concept of *tikkun olam* appears in Judaism in various periods, and the different meanings it had are not similar to the accepted meaning today. For example, the Mishnah and the Gemara (*Gittin* 4:5) stipulate that "one should not ransom captives for more than their value because of *tikkun olam*"—namely, an exaggerated ransom should not be paid for captives so there won't be an incentive to abduct more of them.

464 Theodor Herzl wrote that in his diary on June 14, 1895. Naama Carmi compared the concepts of "Altneuland" and "Utopia." Herzl believed that the Jewish State should serve as a model state for the rest of mankind.

465 I've intentionally avoided getting into a discussion about the interpretative aspects of the mission argument—and specifically, to what extent that argument can rely on Jewish sources. The Torah contains no clear message about a mission, apart from a few of a general nature. The writings of the Prophets address it at greater length, but there, too, the message requires scrupulous interpretation. Yair Sheleg ("Passover Comes Before Shavuot," *Makor Rishon*, May 17, 2012 [Hebrew]}, reasonably argued that "the idea of a future, national and universal redemption first appears in the books of the Latter Prophets: Isaiah, Jeremiah, Ezekiel, and others of their generation who are included in the Minor Prophets. The timing is not coincidental: the winds of the destruction are already blowing, the Kingdom of Israel has been destroyed, and the Kingdom of Judah is faltering and according to some of those prophets, has already collapsed. To counter that disaster-filled present, it was necessary to offer a future of redemption. Given the context, the vision of redemption that was formulated should be perceived in its universal sense. To counter the present state of the Jews as a people who had been humiliated by nations stronger than them, the idea of redemption emerges and paints an optimistic horizon that not only pertains to the condition of the Jews themselves, but also to their status in the world: when redemption comes, the Jews and their religion will be the focus of admiration by all mankind." There are, however, some thinkers (such as Sacks) who believe that the mission was embedded in the Torah already from the start.

466 For a review of the concept of *tikkun olam* and its possible meanings, see: Avi Sagi, *Tikkun Olam Between Utopian Idea and Socio-Historical Process*, Brill, 2015. Sagi leans towards the interpretation that restricts the needed "repair" in the world to an act which is not intended to bring utopian stability to the existing reality. He also highlights the fundamental difference between Judaism and Christianity as regards this matter. See also: Avi Sagi, *The Human Voyage to Meaning: A Philosophical-Hermeneutical Study of Literary Works*, Bar-Ilan University Press, 2009, 176–200. (See chapter 6.) Some have found different biblical sources for *tikkun olam*, including the sacrifice of seventy bulls during the Sukkot holiday. According to the Talmud, the bulls were offered as a sacrifice "for the seventy nations of the world" (Babylonian Talmud, *Sukkah,* 55b). The Talmud even explains that "Woe to the Gentiles who have lost so much without realizing what they lost. When the Temple was standing, the altar atoned for them, and now there is no one to atone for them." Based on that explanation, the sacrifice of the bulls in the Temple was done for the rest of the nations of the world—an act of universal responsibility.

467 Bondi, 283.

468 David S. Ariel, What Do Jews Believe?: The Spiritual Foundations of Judaism. Schocken Books, 1995. 108–134.

469 Edmond Fleg, *Why I Am a Jew*, trans. Louise Waterman Wise. Bloch Publishing, 1945. Fleg wrote: "There are two aspects of this mission. To proclaim throughout

the earth the Name of the One God. To hope, to wait, and to work toward the end that with the coming of the Messiah, justice and peace shall reign on earth."

470 Ein Ayah Berakhot, 8a [Hebrew].

471 Dubnow, 40.

472 Martin Buber, "The Holy Way," in *On Judaism*, ed. Nahum N. Glatzer. Schocken Books, 1967, 108–148. See also: Michael Graetz, "Secular Messianism in the Nineteenth Century as a Way Back to Judaism," in *Messianism and Eschatology*, ed. Zvi Baras. Zalman Shazar Center, 1983, 401–418, [Hebrew]. Buber talks about "the historical mission of the Jewish people, namely an ideal which is no other than the dominion of God on the face of the earth."

473 Leora Batnitzky, Idolatry and Representation: The Philosophy of Franz Rosenzweig Reconsidered. Princeton University Press, 2000, 91.

474 See: Ofer Shiff, "Abba Hillel Silver and David Ben-Gurion: A Diaspora Leader Challenges the Revered Status of the 'Founding Father,'" *Studies in Ethnicity and Nationalism* 10 (2010), 391–421. And also Zohar Segev, "The Jewish State in Abba Hillel Silver's Overall World View," *American Jewish Archives Journal* 56 (2004).

475 David Ben-Gurion, "An Exemplary State: Goal and Means," in *Vision and Path V*. Am Oved, 1958, 78–81 [Hebrew].

476 Ben-Gurion, 78.

477 The historian Nir Mann had the following to say about that: "When Ben-Gurion, on behalf of the proclaimed State of Israel, faced the nations of the world, he underscored, starting from the opening line, the special standing of the Jewish people over the generations: a standing that embodies a sense of inner superiority." See: Nir Mann, *The Zionist Movement and the Idea of the "Exemplary Society."* Institute for Zionist Strategies, 2011 [Hebrew].

478 Leonard Fein: "The Jewish Mission: We are the Witnesses," *The Forward*, March 3, 2010.

479 Grinstein, 65.

480 Sacks, *Future Tense*, 247.

481 The Dreyfuss quote is from an article by Avi Beker that appeared in *Haaretz* on March 2, 2006, entitled "Dancing for Tikkun Olam." Beker's book, *Who is the Chosen People?: The Biggest Struggle of Ideas in History* (Yedioth Ahronoth Books, n.d., Hebrew) deals with the concept of chosenness and the obligations it imposes on the Jewish people. Beker chose to underscore the view which posits that the Jews' chosenness as a people made them emissaries without asking them first if they agree.

482 Their chosenness doesn't give the Jews an "advantage." Rather, it places a burden on them, as Prager and Telushkin wrote in their celebrated book. Dennis Prager and Joseph Telushkin, *The Nine Questions People Ask About Judaism*, Simon & Schuster, 1986, 112. (First published in 1975.) It's worth noting that the Jews are just one of many peoples who believe they were chosen to play a role in the

global drama. The United States rests on a tradition of "exceptionalism" that has been regularly articulated by its leaders, from George Washington to Barack Obama. The same holds true for France, as well as Russia and Poland, Serbia and Iran—every people, every tradition and its own version of chosenness.

483 For more about the roots of *tikkun olam* among American Jews, see Rosner, *Shtetl, Bagel, Baseball*, 99. Shlomo Bardin, who was apparently the first to use the term in its current meaning, believed that the *Aleinu LeShabeach* prayer is the most important expression of Jewish values.

484 Leon Pinsker, *Auto-Emancipation*, 1882. A 1935 translation is available online.

485 This quote from Brenner appeared in Assaf Sagiv, "Not Normal," *Azure* 11 (2001). In his article, Sagiv presents some cogent arguments: "It cannot be denied, then, that the normalizing tendency within Zionism has been a part of the movement more or less from the beginning. Yet it is a distortion of history to argue, as have some of Pinsker's and Brenner's radicalized ideological descendants of late, that these views reflected the mainstream of classic Zionist thought." Sagiv further added: "…the dominant approach…saw the Jewish national movement as motivated by dreams that went far beyond 'normalization.'…"

486 A. B. Yehoshua, *Between Right and Right*, Doubleday, 1981. In response to the Hebrew edition of the book *In Praise of Normality*, Professor Yehezkel Dror wrote an article, "In Denunciation of Normality." Dror rejected many of Yehoshua's premises and maintained that the desire for normality is a form of idolatry and is contrary to the radical nature of the Jewish people. See: Yehezkel Dror, "In Denunciation of Normality," *Kivunim* 45, 7–19 [Hebrew].

487 See, for example, the article written by Ran Baratz, who rejects the demand that Israel be an "exemplary" society: "Israel is not a Jewish, religious, left-wing, right-wing, or universal utopian fantasy—or any combination thereof. The State of Israel has no, nor will have, any 'exemplary' type justification." Ran Baratz, "Light Unto the Nations, Darkness Unto the Jews," *Mida*, September 7, 2015 [Hebrew].

488 Yair Sheleg (op. cit.) claimed that, in its current format, it's a "modern Jewish enterprise" of those who "abandoned the tradition of their forefathers—at least by a half, a third, or a quarter."

489 Examples can be found in: Dov Schwartz, *Religious Zionism between Logic and Messianism*. Am Oved, 1999 [Hebrew]. It's also worth reading Micah Goodman's explanation of the Jews' choice in *The Dream of the Kuzari*. See: Micah Goodman, *The Dream of the Kuzari*, Dvir, 2012, 137 [Hebrew].

490 Traces of that controversy can also be found in an ongoing debate about whether overly strict observance of the Commandments erodes the Jews' moral fiber. The biblical prophets alluded to that and, nowadays, some critics contend that Jewish orthodoxy is preoccupied with rituals at the expense of a universal human and moral sensitivity, which is more important. However, that kind of a debate has been going on for centuries, either among the Jews themselves, or

between Jews and non-Jews. Actually, some of the grievances that Jesus had in his day against the Pharisees were of a similar nature. (See, for example, David Flusser, *Jesus*, Magnes Press, 1997).

491 See: Zeev Levy, *Spinoza and the Concept of Judaism*, Sifriat Hapoalim, 1983 [Hebrew]. Spinoza's considerable influence was also felt in the Jewish circles that washed their hands of his "heresy" and continued to denounce him for abandoning Judaism and the Jewish people. Levy writes: "In his analysis of the Spinoza affair and Spinoza's ideas, even the greatest of all modern Jewish historians, Zvi Heinrich Graetz, was unable to overcome his preconceptions about Spinoza and described him as a 'Jew hater.' However, in his letters to Moses Hess, Graetz wrote that both of them are Spinoza enthusiasts—Hess 100%, and he himself, 75%." (p. 12).

492 Deutsch and Nicgorski, 52.

Acknowledgments

Writing this book compelled me to enter into a long and fascinating period of reading and reflection. Having relied on hundreds of books and articles, I owe a debt of gratitude to the thinkers and researchers I learned and quoted from. Their names appear in the detailed list of endnotes and references.

I wish to thank the people at Anu, The Museum of the Jewish People, who sent me on this mission: Irina Nevzlin, the chair of the board of directors, and Dan Tadmor, the former CEO (and currently, President and CEO of the Weitzman National Museum of American Jewish History). Both stood by me through the entire process and served as an important sounding board when arranging the ideas I wanted to convey.

I thank the team at JPPI, where I have worked as a Senior Fellow since 2010. Professor Yedidya Stern, the president of JPPI, and Dr. Shuki Friedman, the CEO, deserve my gratitude for tolerating me and supporting the book's publication. I also wish to thank the indefatigable project manager of JPPI, Ita Alkalai; Barry Geltman, JPPI's English Language Editor, whose support and help made this volume possible; and former JPPI president, Avinoam Bar Yosef, who made a bet on a younger but no less Jewishly annoying Fellow.

I am grateful to Talia Avnon-Benveniste, Peter Berkowitz, Orit Shaham Gover, Micah Goodman and Shlomo Fischer; and especially to Dr. Shalom Wald, and Shlomo Rosner, for reviewing and making corrections to the manuscript and enriching me with their constructive comments.

I have great admiration for Marilyn Fefer, who translated the Hebrew manuscript into English without causing me any heartache along the way. And to Jessica Kasmer-Jacobs for editing the English manuscript and assisting with the process of needed updates. The Jews are an ancient people, but the last decade proved to necessitate alterations in tone and content.

I extend my appreciation to the team at Kinneret Zmora-Bitan Dvir Publishers, the publisher of the Hebrew version of the book; and also to Imri Zartal and Sarit Rosenberg. I wish to thank Chaya Ekstein for assisting me in the research and production logistics.

And to my family, who had to contend with the burden that every writer places on those closest to him. I wish to thank my children, Shaul, Yochai, Ariel, and Yael; and my wife, Orna Landau, whose husband's heart trusted.

About the Author

Photo by: Amit Naim

Shmuel Rosner is a Tel Aviv–based researcher, columnist, and editor. He is a longtime Senior Fellow at The Jewish People Policy Institute (JPPI), and a weekly columnist for *The Jewish Journal* in LA and *Maariv* in Israel. He has written regularly for *The New York Times*, *The Jerusalem Post*, *Slate*, *Commentary*, and his work has also appeared in *Foreign Policy*, *The New Republic*, *The Jewish Review of Books*, and others. Rosner's previous book is *#IsraeliJudaism: Portrait of a Cultural Revolution* (2019).